MY LIFE
GROWING UP ON A FARM

RONALD D. SNEE

For Luc, my favorite Grandson

May writing your memories give you much joy

Grandpa

Copyright © 2023 by Ronald D. Snee

All rights reserved. This book or any portion thereof may not be reproduced or used in any manner whatsoever without the express written permission of the publisher except for the use of brief quotations in a book review.

ISBN: 9798394948183 (Paperback)

Design and publishing assistance by The Happy Self-Publisher.

TABLE OF CONTENTS

Preface. vii

Chapter 1: So Where is Amity Anyway?. 1

Chapter 2: Early Memories. 7

Chapter 3: Elementary School 1947-54 13

Chapter 4: Methodist Church and the Fireman's Hall 23

Chapter 5: Our Neighbors and the Surrounding Area 27

Chapter 6: Amity and Beyond 33

Chapter 7: Mealtime 35

Chapter 8: Our Nannies 37

Chapter 9: Movies, Trips and Visits to the Farm. 41

Chapter 10: Animal Husbandry 47

Chapter 11: Hunting, Fishing and Trapping 63

Chapter 12: Spring and Summer 67

Chapter 13: Fall and Winter 73

Chapter 14: Baseball with Sam Cooper and Mr. Bristor. 79

Chapter 15: Lessons in Biology – Flora and Fauna 83

Chapter 16: Trinity High School 1955-1959 85

Chapter 17: College Years 1959-1963 89

Chapter 18: My Early Years of Employment 99

Chapter 19: Our Vehicles 103

Chapter 20: Lessons Learned 107

Chapter 21: Leaving the Farm 109

Epilogue 111

Acknowledgements 113

About the Author 115

DEDICATION

In memory of my parents, Rolland Davis and Helene Weber Snee. They provided leadership, guidance, and support for the many educational, farm and business experiences I describe contained in this book. I am indeed very thankful for the wonderful life I had growing up on the farm.

To my wife Marge who listened many times to the stories contained herein. Her patience, understanding, and encouragement went well beyond what was reasonable to expect.

PREFACE

This book is about my life growing up on a farm in Amity, Pennsylvania, from 1945 to 1963. My intention is to capture the key events, document my early life, share the experiences I had, what we learned and how I became the man I am today. Unique experiences are explored. It's a personal perspective that is intended to relate my experiences, not necessarily those of others.

I hasten to add that my formative years were very good years and I look back on my life on the farm with great pride and joy. There is very little I would change if I had it to do over again.

The time period covered is from first grade in 1947 at Amity School, a two-room schoolhouse, to graduation from Washington and Jefferson College in 1963. There was no kindergarten in those days. The setting is southwestern Pennsylvania in Washington and Greene Counties.

It was a time of great transition. The principal industries were steel, glass, coal mining and farming. Farming was on the downturn and many residents combined farming with other occupations. One cannot be a successful farmer without loving the land and the life it provides. This is why many chose to continue farming while finding other means to supplement their income.

Jerry Apps, a noted author who has written extensively on farm life said it well: "Do your chores without complaining. Show up on time. Do every job well. Always try to do better. Never stop learning. Next year will be better. Care for others, especially those who have less than you. Accept those who are different from you. Love the land."

Learning began with four grades in one room. This was supplemented by learning biology from the flora and fauna of the farm, breeding prize winning purebred Hampshire sheep, raising crops, the vagaries of the weather—including heavy rains and extended droughts—and flooding of Ten Mile Creek.

Being active in 4-H for six years taught me about leading projects to successful completion, including project reports and profit and loss statements. This was my introduction to the realities of competition and the business world.

Along the way, I had the privilege of being educated by some great teachers. I also learned from others in my one room school by listening to the more advanced grades recite and in high school by listening to fellow students studying in groups for exams.

Documenting this very important time in my life was a great joy for me. I hope that you, my readers, gain enjoyment reading about what a rich life growing up on the farm can be.

CHAPTER 1

SO WHERE IS AMITY ANYWAY?

Amity is a little town tucked away in southwest Pennsylvania on US Route 19 thirty-five miles directly north of Morgantown, West Virginia, and forty-five miles directly south of Pittsburgh, Pennsylvania. A better way to find Amity is to approach it as the settlers did when they moved west from Cumberland, Maryland, on what is now US Route 40. A former animal and Indian trail, Route 40 winds through western Maryland, turning northwest into southwestern Pennsylvania. It moves up and down hills and through valleys, passing George Washington's Fort Necessity near Uniontown, then into Washington and west into Wheeling, West Virginia, and further points west, terminating in Utah. Route 40 was the main route west in early colonial days.

Route 40 intersects Route 19 in Washington, the county seat of Washington County. In addition to the courthouse are Washington and Jefferson (W&J) College, the Jessop and Washington Steel Mills, the Hazel-Atlas and Duncan Miller glass plants, and a variety of supporting small businesses.

Historically, Washington passed its peak in the fifties and sixties with the decline of the coal, steel and glass industries. The area is the location

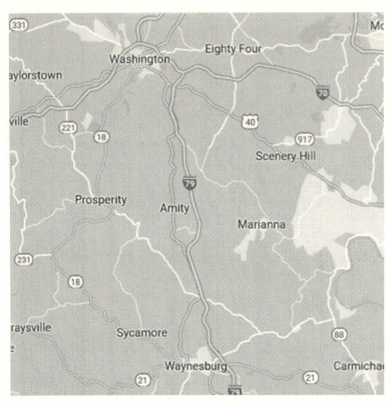

Map of Southwestern PA showing the location of Amity in relation to Pittsburgh, Washington and Waynesburg

of the infamous 1791-94 Whiskey Rebellion, a violent anti-tax uprising led by farmers. W&J, my alma mater, was founded in 1781 and is the oldest college west of the Allegheny Mountains and the eleventh oldest college in the nation.

The inhabitants of the area were coal miners, glass and steel mill workers, and farmers, many of whom also worked in the mines and mills. My mother and father moved to Washington from the Pittsburgh area in 1935, when my father started Snee Dairy, a business that he and my mother operated until their retirement in 1970.

To find Amity, take Route 19 out of Washington and travel south for about thirteen miles. The Snee farm is a couple of miles south of Amity.

This is the route Mom and Dad took to and from their business after they moved to the farm in 1945. It's the same route our school bus traveled to take my siblings and me to Trinity High School in Washington for education, dances and dates. And it is the route I traveled to W&J, hitchhiking my freshman year and later commuting by pickup truck. While we lived on the farm south of Amity, my parents' livelihood and much of our activity was centered in Washington.

After exiting Washington through its suburb, Laboratory, Route 19 meanders down a long valley, with lush green hills to the right and left. There are pastures grazed by beef and dairy cattle. Four miles along is Dan Day Hill, where a twisting road travels up the hill about a half-mile and around a sharp lefthand curve at the top. This is the top of Amity Ridge, and seven miles down the road is Amity. Along the way are green pastures, cornfields and forests.

On this road are Runyon's store, which was well known for Mrs. Runyon's apple pie; a service station, the Ice Cream Cone, where we got hot dogs and ice cream cones in the summer; Jackson's Apple Orchard, where we got delicious cider each fall; Ross' Tavern; and the new Amity Elementary School. At the end of the ridge is Amity. Along the ridge, Route 19 winds up and down and could be quite difficult to maneuver in the winter when it snowed. More about this later.

Signs posted at both ends of the town state that Amity is the Town of Friendly Relationships, which was true for the most part. The town dates back to 1797 and is approximately two miles in length, bordering both sides of Route 19. Amity has a small grocery store; a Presbyterian Church; a Veteran's Memorial; the Fireman's Hall—home of the Amity Volunteer Fire Company—my old two-room schoolhouse that closed in 1951; the Methodist Church, of which my family were members; the US Post Office that served Amwell Township; and two auto repair garages. One was Mankey Brothers Garage, which also sold new Chevrolets and Fords. Amity was home to approximately 1500 people and 350 to 400 houses.

The south end of Amity on Route 19 is the beginning of the descent from Amity Ridge down Amity Hill, passing Winnett's ball field—where all the Amity baseball teams played over the years—and crossing Ten Mile Creek to the Ten Mile–Marianna Road. A left turn on this road, followed by crossing the creek again and immediately turning left was the driveway to Snee Farm.

Ten Mile Creek wraps around the Snee Farm on two sides and was central to many activities. At an early age, we liked to say you could follow Ten Mile Creek to New Orleans, Louisiana. The creek has its headwaters not far from the farm. It continues flowing until it reaches the Youghiogheny River, which flows into the Monongahela River, meeting the Allegheny River in Pittsburgh to form the Ohio River that flows into the Mississippi River and terminates at the Gulf of Mexico in New Orleans. So it was possible to put a boat in at the Snee Farm and in a few months, arrive in New Orleans. How's that for a geography lesson?

Instead of turning off Route 19 to get to our farm, there was the Midway Bar (Rinky Dinks). After about a half-mile, the road travels up a hill to Greene County, which is directly south of Washington County and is bordered by West Virginia on the South. And so it goes in western

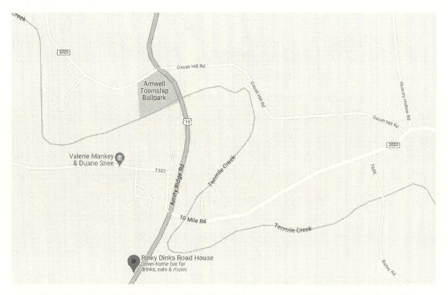

Map showing the location of the Snee Farm south of Amity. The farm is triangular in shape, with Ten Mile Creek on two sides and the Youngman-Vorhees property on the other side

Pennsylvania: up and down hills, through valleys between hills and across the top of ridges on winding roads.

There were two covered bridges in the area nearby. The Bailey Bridge was down the road from the farm in the direction of the village of Ten

Covered bridge at Snee Farm crossing Ten Mile Creek. This bridge was later replaced with a steel bridge

Bailey Bridge east of the Snee Farm (see map in picture 2. This bridge is today the site of the annual Covered Bridge Festival.

Mile. The Bailey Bridge allowed us to cross Ten Mile Creek to get to the Bailey Farm. The Bailey Bridge stands today and is the site of the annual Covered Bridge Festival in Amwell Township. The other bridge was on Ten Mile Road near Route 19. It crossed Ten Mile Creek and led to Snee Farm, Ten Mile, and Marianna. This covered bridge was replaced sometime in the 1920's or 1930's with a steel bridge known to me only by photos.

CHAPTER 2

EARLY MEMORIES

I was born in Washington Hospital in Washington, Pennsylvania, on December 11, 1941. My brothers Tom and Duane were born in the same hospital in 1943 and 1945. My mother and father were born and raised in Homestead and Pleasant Hills, respectively, which are suburbs of Pittsburgh. They married in 1934 and moved to Washington in 1935, when my dad started Snee Dairy. The Snee family had been in the United States since 1792, when Thomas Snee, my great-great-great grandfather immigrated to Jefferson Township—outside of Pittsburgh—from Ireland.

We lived in an apartment above Snee Dairy at 766-68 West Chestnut Street in Washington. My father constructed the building as a home for the dairy. I remember very little of those early years except looking out the window onto Route 40—known then and today in Washington as West Chestnut Street—and wishing I could go outside and play. That was, of course, out of the question, as West Chestnut Street was a major highway that ran right through the center of town. In the sixties, Route 70 was constructed parallel to Route 40, bypassing Washington, much to the pleasure of those traveling east and west through the area. The downside was that many businesses suffered from the decrease in visitors that no longer traveled through the city.

My parents purchased our farm in 1943. It was a total of thirty acres in Amwell Township near Amity, fifteen miles south of Washington, a quarter mile off Route 19 on the Ten Mile-Marianna Road. The cost was five thousand dollars. They purchased our home from a Pittsburgh family that used the property as a summer and weekend retreat. At one time, the farm was used to grow and sell gladiolas. The front lawn was full of them.

Mom and Dad moved to the farm in 1945 after an indoor bathroom was installed. Mom wouldn't move to the farm otherwise. I remember using the outhouse a few times. It was subsequently torn down and the site was used to burn garbage.

The farmhouse was built in the early to mid-1800's. It was two stories, with a kitchen, living room, dining room and maid's room on the first floor. The second floor consisted of two bedrooms, a bathroom and a small office area. Mom and Dad had one bedroom. My brothers and I shared the other bedroom, with Tom and I in one bed and Duane in the other.

A gas furnace heated the house. The gas was piped in from a meter about a half-mile away on the Ross Swart farm near the old Swart School House, which had been converted into a home. This was significant, as in

Snee Farmhouse (Circa 1940's) was built in the mid-1800s.

the winter, Dad would have to thaw the frozen gas line. Sometime after I left for Rutgers in 1963, Dad replaced the furnace with a wood-fired furnace that was supplemented with electric heat. The heat was turned off at night for safety reasons and it got very cold in the bedrooms in the winter. It wasn't unusual to wake up in the morning and see our breath. On those days, we moved quickly when getting out of bed!

The grounds around the house were nicely done with many pine trees and shrubs. Dad liked pines and planted several over the years. He particularly liked hemlocks. The lawn consisted of about two acres in the front and a half-acre in the rear.

As far back as I can remember, Mom worked in the business and also took care of financial matters. Mom had expertise with finance, having a business degree from Duff's Iron City College in 1929 and working in the area prior to starting Snee Dairy with my father. When Dad went to the farm, Mom made the ice cream and ran the business. She made breakfast in the morning, packed lunches, got us off to school and then went to work. She did the food shopping once a week and cooked dinner in the evening. She had a series of cleaning ladies to help with the cleaning and other housework. Once a week, she would get her hair and nails done in Washington at Blod Fox's beauty parlor. I went to high school with Blod's daughter, Judy Fox. Mom didn't really like the farm but tolerated it. Dad liked it and thought it was a good place to raise us boys.

Mom and Dad: Rolland Davis and Helene Weber Snee on their wedding day in 1934

Dad liked to work the farm and in the middle to late 1950's, he worked there full time. He liked to grow things. Dad wasted a lot of money on the farm, and it was up to Mom to make ends meet. He was always experimenting on the farm and trying something new. Making money was not an objective. She did a great job at running the business. Dad claimed Mom did a great job but couldn't make the big decisions. He had to make the big decisions and he didn't shrink from the opportunity.

Dad returned to the ice cream business in the late 1950's, delivering ice cream door to door. He had daily delivery routes Monday through Saturday in parts of Washington and Greene counties. When reading *Growing Up in Eighty Four, Pennsylvania* by Keith Neill, I was amazed to read, "I don't know how he knew, but Mr. Snee, who drove an ice cream delivery truck, started coming to our house. All the neighborhood kids called him The Ice Cream Man. Now the ice cream shop came to our back door." That Ice Cream Man was my father. Eighty Four is a few miles east of Washington.

Both my mother and father enjoyed working. My dad retired to the farm and was active in gardening until his death at eighty-seven. After retiring from the ice cream business, my mother went to work as an accountant for my brothers' dental practice. She took early retirement at seventy-seven. She had a sign above her desk which read "Old accountants never die. They just become unbalanced."

My dad had a strong interest in politics and was a rabid Republican, as were several Snees. One cousin, Sylvester Snee, who was a brother of my grandfather, was elected judge of common pleas court in Pittsburgh. This was quite a feat, as Pittsburgh is a Democratic city. His son John subsequently made an unsuccessful run for district attorney.

Dad would vote early in the morning on Election Day and never missed voting as far as I know. It taught me the importance of voting and I've tried to follow his example.

Many spirited political discussions were had over the years. Dad was known to voice strong feelings on everything political, as well as other subjects. He did support at least one Democrat, Bus Andrews, for township road supervisor. Dad said it was okay to support a Democrat at the local level.

Bus Andrews was also the town barber. Haircuts were a dollar; nothing fancy, but he got the job done. He cut hair in the living room of his house. There were often six or seven men and boys waiting. Lots of high-spirited and energetic discussions were known to take place. It's interesting to note that NPR has a radio show called the *Barbershop* that focuses on the issues of the day.

I don't recall when, but at some point, we decided to get our hair cut in town, certainly by high school years, maybe sooner.

CHAPTER 3

ELEMENTARY SCHOOL 1947-54

I attended two Amity Schools. The first was in the middle of Amity across from the Methodist Church. I went to this school from first grade to midway through fifth grade, 1947-52, when we started going to the new Amity school, which I attended from 1952-54. The first school consisted of two rooms. Grades 1 through 4 were downstairs and were taught by Mrs. Freda B. Elliott. Grades 5 through 8 were upstairs and were taught by Miss Rita L. Carroll. There was no library and no school nurse; our two teachers did it all.

Prior to going to school, I was required to get a smallpox vaccination. This was given by Dr. Dodd, who resided in Amity and made house calls all over Amwell Township and elsewhere. Dr. Dodd was well known and was a respected member of the community. He was also known for his Indian artifacts collection, which was a great treat to see. I was told that many of the arrowheads in his collection were found on my parents' farm many years ago. My brothers and I enjoyed walking over the freshly plowed fields looking for arrowheads. We found several.

I remember the two-story Amity School and the happy times I had there. Instead of a drinking fountain, there was a hand-operated water pump out front. We would take turns pumping the water while the rest of us filled our drinking cups in the morning before school, at recess and during the lunch period. As we entered the building, the cloakroom was on the right.

Amity School #1 had two rooms: grades 1-4 downstairs and grades 5-8 upstairs. The water fountain was a well with a pump handle in the front. The outhouses were in the rear
Photo Courtesy of Amwell Township Historical Society Collection

It was there that we hung our coats and stored our lunches and drinking cups. Mrs. Elliott's desk was at the front of the room beyond the cloakroom. Behind her desk—high on the wall—was a picture of George Washington, the first president of the United States and father of our country, as we were told. I learned much later in life that George Washington owned much of the land we now know as southwestern Pennsylvania.

On Mrs. Elliott's desk was a bottle of Airwick on one corner. The piano and platform were to the left as we faced the rear of the room where the stove was. On the other corner of Mrs. Elliott's desk was a big bell that she used to signal the end of recess and lunchtime. She also used it to initiate fire drills, a scary experience for a first grader. Mrs. Elliott had to ring the bell very loudly so that Miss Carroll's second floor classroom would hear it. Mrs. Elliott used the bottle of Airwick to counteract unpleasant odors that often permeated the classroom.

Facing the building was the Fireman's Hall to the left and the playground to the right and rear. The only bathrooms were outhouses located behind the school, one for boys and one for girls. On several occasions, the older kids

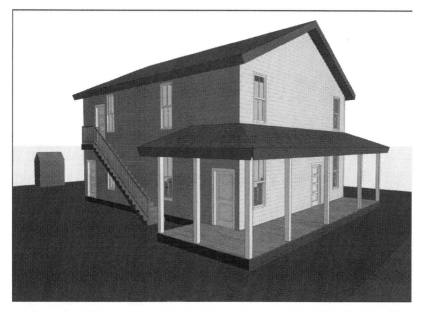

Schematic of the outside of Amity School #1 created by Michelle Linville

Schematic of the inside of Amity School #1 created by Michelle Linville

upset the outhouses on Halloween. In the winter, we would ride sleds down the big hill behind the outhouses.

Heat came from a coal-fired potbellied stove in the rear of the room that heated both the first and second floors. Paul Elliott, Mrs. Elliott's husband, came to school early each cold morning to start the fire. We were always warm. He would open the building, fire up the stove and get the room ready for Mrs. Elliott and her students. I've always thought of them as a team and rarely saw them apart. I also remember going to school with the Elliott children, Joan and Paul, and attending baseball games in which Paul played with my brothers, Tom and Duane. Joan was one year older than me; Paul was my brother Duane's age.

School was fun and we learned many things in addition to the material in our books. Mrs. Elliott told me once not to waste time because every moment wasted was gone forever, never to return. This is a lesson I've never forgotten. We also found we could learn from the older students by listening to them recite instead of studying. Such a helpful distraction is easy when there are four grades in a single room.

It was during first grade arithmetic that I found I needed glasses. We recited arithmetic by answering questions on flash cards while standing on the platform at the side of the room. I was getting poor grades in arithmetic. One day, Mrs. Elliott stood closer, and I answered the questions correctly. I told Mrs. Elliott that I could see the cards better when she stood closer. She told my mother and an eye exam showed that I needed glasses. I got straight As in arithmetic after that.

I remember my first written arithmetic test on which the last and toughest question was "Color three ducks yellow" out of a possible six. I answered all the problems correctly. I was very proud of my achievement and my mother retained this test in my scrapbook.

There were approximately fifty students per room, twelve to thirteen per grade. Usually, one grade was taught at a time, while the other three grades studied. In second and third grades, I enjoyed listening to the third and fourth grades recite to see which answers I knew. Mrs. Elliott played the piano, and we sang songs. Each day began with the pledge of allegiance to the flag and the Lord's Prayer. There was a Halloween party and a

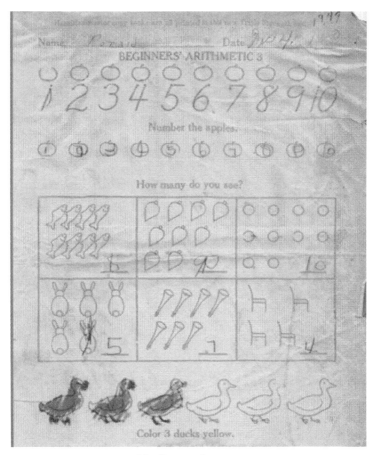

My first math exam

Christmas party that often included a play by the students. We exchanged valentines. Play outside at recess included baseball and football and sled riding down the steep hill in the field behind the schoolhouse. We brought our sleds to school on the school bus.

The classroom was laid out in four quadrants, with the teacher in the front. Facing the front of the room, the grades were assembled in the quadrants. First grade was front left; second grade was back left; third grade was back right; and fourth grade was front right. Each year, we could count on the first grade missing a week with the chicken pox and the second grade missing a week with the measles. This was our first lesson in infectious diseases. We didn't study it; we experienced it.

In our school district, children didn't go to kindergarten. The children I remember that were in my first-grade class were Duane Winnett, Ruthann Golsky, Norma Brown, Jane Bird and Bette Lea McAfee. J. D. Frazee joined the group at the new school. This group and others went through high school together.

We learned the thrill and anxiety of competition as we answered arithmetic flashcard problems and spelled words while lined up as a class on the platform. We recited spelling and arithmetic on a foot-high platform at the left side of the room facing the rear of the room. The process was effective. Each student was asked to spell a word or answer an arithmetic question. If the student gave the wrong answer, the student next in line could answer the question. If the second student gave the correct answer, he or she moved ahead of the student that previously missed the question.

When the recitation period was over, students with the most correct answers were at the head of the class, and the ones who gave the fewest right answers were at the bottom of the class. It was easy to see where you stood in class ranking. I wonder if reciting in this way in country schools was where the terms head and bottom of the class originated.

On one occasion, Mrs. Elliott used a unique approach to change student behavior. In first grade, each student was given a big pencil that contained a thick black lead. The pencil was placed on the top of each student's desk in a grooved pencil holder near the top of the desk. One of the students insisted on chewing on her pencil. Over time, she needed a new pencil sooner than the other students. driving up costs as well as being unhealthy.

Mrs. Elliott took her chewed pencil away and replaced it with the biggest spike I have seen, then or today. The spike rested on the top of the desk for all to see. The student was instructed to "Chew on this spike if chew you must." After a few days of embarrassment, the pencil returned to the top of the desk. There was no more chewing after that. I wonder if such an intervention would be allowed today.

My first-grade picture is a classic: thick glasses and a safety pin for the button on my shirt. The button was off, and Mom replaced it with a safety pin on the day I had my school picture taken.

We rode the bus to school. Raymond (Peck) Gaus was the bus driver for all eight years of my elementary school. With a nickname like Peck, he was ribbed relentlessly over the years. On the first day of school, I wore short pants and got kidded a lot. I told Mom, and I wore long pants after that. We took our lunch to school in a pail or brown bag. For the first few days, Mom gave me ham sandwiches. I mentioned to her that the other kids had bologna sandwiches. She switched to bologna, and I got bologna sandwiches for the next twelve years clear through high school!

My first-grade picture

The first Amity School was a very enjoyable experience. I've always felt that I had an educational advantage and enjoy relating my experiences to others. It's difficult for people to believe I went to a two-room school and continued to stay in touch with my first-grade teacher until her passing. I'm convinced that the world would be a much better place if teachers understood the profound influence they have on the lives of their students and took their jobs as seriously and with as much enthusiasm and dedication as Mrs. Elliott.

In fifth grade, we moved upstairs to be taught by Miss Rita L. Carroll. This was a big deal. Miss Carroll was older, stern and not as much fun as Mrs. Elliott, although she was a great teacher. In 1952, the second semester of the year, we moved to the new school north of Amity along Route 19. The new school was formed by consolidating somewhere between five and ten small schools. This was my first experience with mergers. The new school was located approximately two miles north of Amity. After more school changes some years later, my second school served as the Amwell Township Administration building.

Shortly after the new school opened, its water well went dry on several occasions. As a result, we had a day off every time the well failed. It seems a little more planning would have avoided this waste of time and embarrassment. The new school had a very large playground in the rear and on the sides of the building. There was enough room for the boys to play baseball in the spring and early fall, followed by touch and sometimes tackle football in late fall. We even had a few teams playing in a league. Unfortunately, there was no sled riding like we had at the two-room school.

One of the downsides of the new school was that the bus ride was longer, with school letting out at 3:30 p.m. and our not getting home until 5:00 p.m. This angered Dad because we couldn't do our chores until late. Dad spoke out to the school board and got some concessions. He was later asked to run for the school board because of his relationship with the officials. He turned the offer down, which disappointed me. I long felt he'd ignored his civic duty.

The new school had eight or nine rooms. Each grade had its own room and teacher. Grades five through eight changed rooms for different subjects. In the new school, I had another favorite teacher, Thelma Roche. She gave me good grades. I also came to respect the principal, Chester Bailey, but I didn't feel as close to him as I did to Mrs. Elliott, Miss Carroll and Mrs. Roche.

I particularly liked Mrs. Elliott. When I got married and started a family, we somehow began exchanging Christmas cards with each other and we continued to do so until she died in her eighties.

I was a good student and the teachers selected me for the American Legion Award as the outstanding eighth grade male student. Ruth Ann Golsky received

My eighth-grade picture taken by Evans Studio in Washington, PA

the award for the outstanding female student. In later years, my brother Duane and several nieces and nephews also received this award.

At eighth grade graduation in 1954, I was on the program reciting the poem *If* by Rudyard Kipling. In classic fashion, I rehearsed and rehearsed. I wanted to do a good job, but I was scared. When it was my turn, I recited the first verse in rapid fire fashion; combined the first half of the second verse with the last half of the third verse; and then finished with all of the fourth verse. I was too scared to stop or slow down. Thankfully, no one said anything about my high-speed performance. Instead, I was congratulated for doing a great job.

For graduation from eighth grade, I was rewarded with my first big, memorable gift: a self-winding, Seth Thomas wristwatch. Mom purchased this brand because it had a good reputation. It was a big deal for me. Mom

Eighth-grade class picture.
Many of these students went on to Trinity High School

took me to a jeweler in Pittsburgh that she knew from her days working in Pittsburgh prior to marrying Dad and moving to Washington.

We went there because Mom knew someone and could get wholesale prices, a lesson I never forgot. I wore that watch from 1954 until sometime in the early 1970's, when I purchased a digital watch for around four hundred dollars. My Seth Thomas still runs to this day, and I use it when the battery in my newer watch dies. I can always count on my Seth Thomas watch. Mom was right!

Mom also had a formal eighth grade picture taken. This gesture made me feel so important and special. I still have that picture in my scrapbook.

CHAPTER 4

METHODIST CHURCH AND THE FIREMAN'S HALL

The Amity Methodist Church is located across the street—US Route 19—from the old Amity School and the fire hall. My parents were members of this church but rarely attended. Dad was too busy, or so he said, so they attended only on rare occasions. My brothers and I were required to attend Sunday school and received many medals and awards for perfect attendance. When we came of age, my brothers and I joined the church. My father was a Methodist and had fond memories of going to a camp as a child with Reverend Debolt. Reverend Debolt baptized my brothers and me in the West Washington Methodist Church even when he belonged to the Amity Church.

As in any small town, many of the kids we went to school with also attended the same church. Mom would take us and then return approximately one hour later to pick us up. She was frequently late and on occasion we would walk home. It was embarrassing to stand around waiting to be picked up and be seen by all your churchgoing friends. I liked going to Sunday school because we were learning something. The Bible was interesting. I had a couple of good teachers, with Ike Crumrine being the most memorable. Ike led one of our most important projects: collecting food and delivering it to needy families on Christmas Eve. This was a very rewarding experience.

We were also members of the Methodist Youth Fellowship. We put on church plays. In one, I played a member of a drill team marching to *Onward Christian Soldiers*, a popular church tune after WWII and during the Korean War. I was pleased to learn that President Eisenhower also liked the song and that it was played at his funeral. Edith Upson played the organ; Freda Elliott played the piano and organ; and Opal Winnett and Polly and Harry Dilly sang in the choir. In June, the church sponsored the Strawberry Festival. This fundraiser was a 'must attend' and was supported by Mom and Dad either by a direct donation of ice cream to be sold or providing the ice cream at a very low cost. Of course, all the neighbors attended.

On the north side of the Methodist Church was the Presbyterian Church. It was a nice big church with a small congregation. We never understood how they met expenses, but they did. While we knew a lot of people in Amity, we knew very few who went to the Presbyterian Church. Both churches shared a big cemetery in which many of the longtime residents are buried, including my mother and father.

On December 25, 1953, Mom and Dad gave me my first Bible. I still have it today, but I must admit that it has not been greatly used. In the back. Mom wrote:

12-25-53

Dear Ronnie: As Daddy and I present this Holy Bible, we have all the thoughts of a boy growing up to be an honorable man. At this presentation, you are twelve years old, attending Sunday school at the Amity Methodist Church: your teacher, Mrs. Robert Lash, your minister, Robert Lash. As years pass by and we may be separated from each other, always remember we dearly love you and your brothers. We always live and hope for your future.

Love,
Mother and Dad

This Bible is a prized possession and serves as a remembrance of my parents. While always busy with work, my mother tried as best she could to be a good mother.

Church was a good experience and I credit what spirituality I have today to my childhood experiences at Amity Methodist Church. I consider myself a lifelong Methodist and regularly attend church when I can.

The fireman's hall stood across from the Methodist Church on the north side of the Amity School. Amity had a volunteer fire company. My parents supported it financially through donations and by providing ice cream for the Fireman's Fair each August. This was a fundraiser that my parents treated in the same fashion as the church's Strawberry Festival. The workings of the firemen were generally unknown to me, as we didn't socialize with the leaders of the organization, which still today enjoys a good reputation in the community.

CHAPTER 5

OUR NEIGHBORS AND THE SURROUNDING AREA

We became good friends with our neighbors over the years. Directly across Ten Mile Creek to the west were Ross and Madeline Swart. They earned their living by farming, although Ross also operated a lumber mill. Ross later sold his farm to the coal company and retired to Amity. Many years later, my brothers bought the farm from the coal company, and Duane actively farms it today. Ross never worked too hard and used to practically sieve his soil before he planted corn. Dad remarked one day that Ross would live to be a hundred years old because he took life so easy. Dad was almost right. Ross died at around ninety years of age. Madeline died much earlier.

A memorable Ross Swart story involved cutting down a Sycamore tree on our property by the creek. The tree was huge and if not felled properly would take down our electric lines. Dad asked Ross for advice because of his expertise as a lumberman. We worked all day getting everything just right per Ross's direction. To make a long story short, the tree came down on the electric lines and we had no electricity for three days—during the winter no less. Ross's reputation as a lumberjack took a beating that day!

Ross took a unique approach to arranging for assisted living in his elder years. This was long before people were in the business of providing assisted living for the elderly. Ross had no family he could depend on to take care of him if needed. He made a deal with a young family in the community that he would pay for adding an apartment onto their house if he could live there until he died. At that time, the apartment would become the property of the young couple. And that was where Ross spent the last years of his life. Such resourcefulness and kindness were characteristic of country folks.

Tommy Farabee lived up the dirt road—Ringland Ridge Road today—from where Ross Swart lived. Tommy could fix anything and frequently helped us when our farm machinery broke down. Tommy was a talker, prompting another farmer, Earl Jackson, to say, "Anyone who talked as much as Tommy couldn't be telling the truth all the time." But Tommy was a good neighbor and gave a lot of assistance to my parents in their later years. Tommy's wife Lenore died in her fifties. Tommy remarried in his middle seventies.

On the north side of the Snee Farm was a farm owned by Mr. Youngman, president of Washington Steel Corporation. His secretary and her husband, Peg and Whitey Vorhees, lived there year round. They were willed the farm when Mr. Youngman died. The Vorhees later sold the farm in the 1970's for a hundred thousand dollars. Whitey said he wanted to see what a hundred thousand dollars looked like all at once. My brothers later tried to purchase the farm but were unsuccessful. It seemed that people from Pittsburgh were bidding up the farm prices.

The Vorhees farm was operated by a series of tenant farmers, the most memorable of which was Vance Litman. Vance pulled horses and chased women. He and his wife Jane were good to us boys. On Saturdays, we would help Vance, and Jane would feed us lunch. Mom and Dad were working, and we were lonesome, so we enjoyed the attention. Vance always had a good team of horses, and he won several pulling contests at county fairs and the Pennsylvania Farm Show.

Vance was one tough farmer. In later years he overturned a tractor and was almost killed. Accidents involving farm machinery and tractors were a common event. Among the most unsafe occupations, farming ranks right up there with mining. He was able to get himself to the hospital and was upset to learn he was in very bad shape and would have to stay in the hospital for several weeks to complete his recovery. Vance told the doctor he'd never been in a hospital before, had no insurance and wasn't going to stay. He went home and recuperated there for the next several weeks. His recovery was remarkable if not miraculous.

At one time on the Swart place, there was an old school that had been converted into a house. Swart rented it to John Gaus and his family and later to others. We went to school with their kids: Johnny, Kay and Nancy, who later moved to Amity. The house was subsequently destroyed by the coal company to reduce taxes, as was the Swart's main house. The coal company bought the farm from Ross Swart who, with his wife Madeline, later retired to Amity. The coal company sold it to my brothers.

The family we spent the most time with and had the greatest influence on us was the Winnetts: Opal, Wally and their children. They were well respected in the community. Their farm was located northwest of ours—up Route 19 toward Amity—about one mile away. There were six children: Sally; Jay, who would take over the lumber business; Mary Lee, who was two years older than me; Duane, who was my age; and Johnny and Donna Mae, who were younger than me.

Wally ran a successful lumber business and a farming operation. Wally was a fun, interesting person to be around. I admired him as the leader of his family. He was a good father, a good husband, a leader in the community, a smart businessman, and a good man! I also admired his independence and his ability to adapt quickly and easily to an ever-changing personal and business world.

I sought Wally out whenever I could because he was fun to be with and learn from. He was always aware of local, national and world events and ready to engage in lively discussion. More importantly, he was interested in what my family and I were doing. I always felt that Wally genuinely cared about us.

My brothers and I did all kinds of things with the Winnetts, particularly with Duane. The foursome—Duane Winnett and the Snees: Tom and

Duane and I—shared sled riding, ice hockey, fox and geese, riding ponies, swimming, school, church and Sunday school. More about this later.

Another character in the area was Herman (Skirmey) Walker. Skirmey, his wife Margret and son Bob lived across Ten Mile Creek from us on a three-to-four-acre plot between the Swart and Winnett properties. He worked at the glass works for many years. Bob was the talk of the area because he didn't get married until his forties and married a woman twenty years his junior.

In the late 1950's, Skirmey moved down Ten Mile-Marianna Road to a farm about three miles from our farm. Mom and Dad bought his previous home and rented it out for many years. Mom loved to tell the story about how during the legal proceedings associated with the property sale, Skirmey amused the lawyer with his directions: "This-a-way, that-a-way, up yonder, down yonder." These were common phrases in the 1950's.

In November of each year, hogs were slaughtered, a prelude to the great homemade sausage Skirmey sold. We always looked forward to the sausage he made when we didn't have our own. Skirmey was a hard worker and could husk field corn and shovel it into the corn crib faster than anyone we knew, even faster than Dad, and that is saying something. He and his son also played on the Amity sandlot baseball team. They would have been in their early twenties and forties, respectively. Bob was a home run threat and Skirmey was a tough out, always getting a lot of singles. He held his own with the young guys.

There were many other neighbors. One was Porter Herrod, a machinist in town who repaired our farm equipment. He introduced us to white lightening, the worst stuff I ever tasted. There was also Red Neigleman, who owned the service station at the top of Greene County hill and was rumored to have dealt in just about any illegal activities you can think of.

The Rinky Dinks bar nearby was called the Midway Rinky Dinks because it was midway between Washington and Waynesburg. In later years it was run by Matt Guza, a famous Waynesburg High School wrestler. He could cook great steaks and barbecued whole and partial sides of beef and pork. The Midway was the watering hole for the local farmers and coal miners. I'll leave the happenings there to the imagination of the reader.

Many a young man got their first drink there. Not many women frequented the place.

There were other neighbors, but the Swarts, Winnetts, Vorhees, Litmans and Farabees—who were our immediate neighbors—were our closest friends in the area. It's clear that as kids we didn't stray too far from home. All our neighbors were honest, hard-working, supportive people we could trust, a rare commodity today.

CHAPTER 6

AMITY AND BEYOND

Communication with the outside world was by means of telephone, newspapers, TV and, of course, personal conversations. Mom and Dad were in Washington on business at least five days a week. In the early years, the telephone was a thirteen-party line run by the Amity Farmers Phone Company. Our ring was two longs and three shorts; Winnett's ring was four shorts. It was not uncommon for people to listen in on each other's conversations.

The operator was Goldie Condit. She lived and operated the switchboard from her house, the former Patterson Hotel, which she operated in the early 1900's. Goldie knew everyone and where they were at any given time. She augmented her neighborhood intelligence by looking out her window onto Route 19. Goldie also served as our 911 operator as well as a general information source. She was often relieved by her daughter, Eleanor Linton, who lived with her family, husband Tom, daughter Nancy and son Tom in the same building. Others, including neighbor Ruthann Golsky, often served as substitute operators.

Later, Ma Bell bought out the Amity phone company and we went to a three- to five party line. Listening in on other's calls continued to be a popular activity. Donna Winnett liked to tell of overhearing my brother Duane describing to one of his friends how my father castrated a cat. Using no anesthetic, the cat was thrust headfirst into a boot. Thus confined, with just his rear and testicles exposed, he couldn't fight or claw anyone. Dad took out his pocketknife, did the operation to the great displeasure of the cat and then turned the cat loose. He survived and went on to live to a ripe old age. This is how things were done on our farm.

Dad was an avid reader of newspapers, and we regularly received the *Pittsburgh Post-Gazette*, *Washington Observer* (mornings) and *Washington Reporter* (evenings). One of the things my brothers and I looked forward to Dad reading us the Sunday funnies. Dad's favorite cartoon strip was Snuffy Smith. I believe he got as much if not more enjoyment out of reading about Snuffy's adventures as my brothers and I did.

The *Observer* and *Reporter* papers were subsequently merged into a single morning newspaper. I got my love of reading newspapers from Dad. It has stayed with me all my life. Interestingly, my daughter Victoria became a TV and radio reporter. She said it was because "she had to know what was going on."

CHAPTER 7

MEALTIME

Meals at the Snee Farm were good, simple (meat and potatoes), filling and healthy. Mom cooked breakfast, packed brown bag lunches for all and prepared dinner in the evening. Mom was a great short order cook and enjoyed feeding visitors.

Dad loved to garden, an activity he pursued until his death at eighty-seven. He raised typical garden fare: tomatoes, potatoes, lettuce, watermelons, cantaloupes, corn, raspberries and strawberries. You name it; he could grow it in abundance. We ate it, canned it and gave it away. In the winter, there was apple cider and sometimes venison in addition to the usual game: pheasant, rabbits, squirrels and an occasional grouse. Everyone who visited the farm—and there were many—left with some homegrown garden produce and sometimes meat, depending on what was available. Dad was happy to do so.

Dad loved to experiment in the garden and try new things. I returned home from Rutgers University one year to find a thirty-foot telephone pole in the middle of the garden with a bean stalk growing about halfway up the pole. When I asked what the purpose was, Dad said, "I just wanted to see how high the bean stalk could get." As I recall, it did get near the top of the pole by the end of summer. Perhaps he recalled the story of *Jack and the*

Beanstalk and wanted to test the theory, even though he never said that was the reason.

Beef and pork were raised on the farm. At Christmastime, Dad would make several varieties of chocolate candy for sale on the ice cream route and for home consumption. Candy was Dad's job. He tried to teach Mom how to make it under the ruse that she needed to know if something happened to him. She had fallen for that ploy once before and wasn't about to let that happen again. That's how she got the job of operating the ice cream making machine!

An important byproduct of mealtime, particularly the evening meal, was the conversation, which was wide-ranging, sometimes contentious and often instructive. Business and business ethics were a common topic, as business was our livelihood and my parents' work. Honesty was of critical importance to my father and mother, my father to a fault. They paid their bills, never beat anyone out of anything and could tell you who in town owed them money. Being in business in Washington since 1935 produced a lot of business dealings, some of which didn't work out to my parents' satisfaction. My business philosophy is deeply rooted in what I learned during those meals and at other times from my parents. Their business philosophy has served me well.

CHAPTER 8

OUR NANNIES

Since my mother worked in the business as chief operating officer and chief financial officer, she hired nannies to help take care of my brothers and me. I have fond memories of three: Mary Onesko, Martha Iams and Edie Wright. Mary Onesko came to work for my parents in the dairy business one or two years before I was born and took care of me from the day I came home from the hospital. She lived near the dairy, came to work in the morning and took care of me all day. When we moved to the farm, Mary couldn't come with us. But she continued to take care of us on special occasions. Mary lived with her elderly mother and had to remain in town to take care of her. Mary continued to work for my parents for more than thirty years until they sold the business in 1970.

When we moved to the farm in 1945, Martha Iams came to live with us and stayed until 1948 or 1949, when she left to marry. Edie Wright took her place. Both Martha and Edie lived in a room behind the kitchen. The wall separating the two rooms was torn down after I left for graduate school in 1963. Edie was sixteen when she started to work for my parents.

Edie stayed for four or five years until she married Howard Crouse. Both Howard and Edie were from Nineveh, which was in Greene County. Howard served as a Marine during the Korean War, and that was when they moved to Nineveh. I recall Howard speeding up our driveway to see Edie when he was home on furlough.

Edith added the following memories to mine. She was our nanny, although we didn't use that term, from August of 1948 through October of 1953. Edie commented:

> "I felt that I must help out with the expenses at home, so I was interviewed by your mother at our home in very rural Greene Co. From the outset of our meeting, we instantly shared a bond of love, your mother and me. I was an undereducated country girl going to work as a nanny for a well-known business family. What a challenge. But I had—still do have—a strong spiritual faith in God.
>
> "Mr. and Mrs. Snee treated me very well with lots of respect and all of you seemed very appreciative of all I did to help. One incident shortly after I started to work for your family happened one morning after you and maybe Tom was in school at the time. Anyway, I had gone out to burn trash and accidentally pulled the kitchen door shut behind me. The night latch was still on. Guess what I did? In desperation, I broke a pane of the glass in the kitchen window and climbed through it. When your mom and dad came home, I was very nervous. But I confessed to them what had happened. Your dad yelled very loudly: We shouldn't have hired someone from Greene County! Hells bells!" I told them to take the price of the window glass out of my pay for that week. Your dad calmed down and said, "We won't make you pay for it; you didn't lie about it.
>
> "Another event I will always remember as follows. Please bear with me. I was taught to cook pretty much country style. I had learned to make homemade bread and you all enjoyed it very much. Your mother usually made a menu for me to follow to cook supper. One morning she left saying to make city chicken for supper, and that all the ingredients were in the fridge.

"I was dumbfounded, needless to say. I said to myself, *A country chicken is the only chicken I know how to cook*. Thank goodness I knew how to read well. Found the recipe in *Better Homes and Gardens Cookbook*, 1945 edition, in the cabinet drawer. It turned out very well; I'm not real sure why. Ha Ha!

"Another story will always be in my memory. There were in your area some "no gooders" as your dad would say. One night we were all in bed and a "rattle trap" kind of car came roaring up the drive and stopped under the apple tree. Your dad raised the bedroom window and thrust a loaded shotgun and yelled to them, "Don't move an inch or I'll blow your heads off," then shot twice in the air. All three of you boys thought that it was hilarious. The next morning, they were still sitting under the apple tree in their car, scared stiff. We all had gone back to sleep; little did we know."

There were several other nannies after Edie and perhaps some in between Edie and Martha, but I don't recall their names. As I reached my early teens, Mom and Dad decided that we no longer needed a nanny—I can't imagine why—and that era ended.

My brothers and I were active, ornery little boys and got into lots of things that created a challenge for our nannies. One time we were in with the hogs, for what reason I can't recall, and got covered with mud. Martha or Edie made us take our clothes off outside the house and she washed us off with cold water from the hose before we were let into the house.

On another occasion, Dad gave us the job of painting the new dump truck bed with creosote, a black chemical used to keep wood from rotting that was widely used on telephone poles and railroad ties. When the job was done, we had creosote all over us, turning much of our skin black. Martha, I believe, scrubbed us clean with Dutch Cleanser, which resulted in large red welts all over our bodies wherever the creosote had been. I don't know which was worse: the creosote or being scrubbed with Dutch Cleanser. Both burnt like hell and the combination was even worse. We were quite a sight, especially when we went to church on Sunday. Either Tom or Duane was in particularly bad shape, with red welts on his face, arms and other parts of his body.

When we were very young, we were accused by one nanny, not one of our favorites, of hiding under the kitchen table and pounding her toes with a hammer.

Mary, Martha and Edie were our favorites and became lifelong friends of the family. Their help and loyalty were very much appreciated.

CHAPTER 9

MOVIES, TRIPS AND VISITS TO THE FARM

My parents weren't much into having fun. They were always too busy making a living or as Mom would tell it, "she was trying to make a dollar out of fifteen cents." In the early fifties, it was a regular Saturday night event to go to the movies at the Wayne Theater in Waynesburg, about ten miles south of Amity on Route 19. My brothers and I loved it. They only showed westerns with stars like Gene Autry, Roy Rogers, Hopalong Cassidy and Lash LaRue. Lash LaRue was quick with a whip as well as a gun. The movies were mostly B grade. The audience was pretty rowdy, with things being thrown during the movie. One time a bag of BBs landed in my lap! It was Saturday night in Greene County and people had a good time!!

Coming from a family of hunters, we were greatly amused by the numerous gunfights. The characters would shoot at each other for a very long time without reloading and never hit anyone. Gunfights were an important part of the movies. On one occasion Duane, still sitting on Dad's knee to see, said. "This movie is no good, Dad. There's not enough shoot'n," loud enough for the whole theater to hear! I never lost my love of westerns and became a big John Wayne fan, although I'm not sure I saw a

John Wayne movie at the Wayne Theater. With the advent of television, we quit going to the movies.

We only took two family vacations that I recall. When I was around ten years old, we went to Deep Creek Lake in Maryland for a week. We even took our nanny, Edie Wright, along. We swam and fished all week. Dad rented a motorboat for fishing. As I recall, we may have caught only one or two fish. But we had a good time, one that I'll long remember.

The other trip I recall was when Dad took us boys to Penn State for a weekend. Mom stayed home. We toured the barns and the fields and admired all the fine crops and animals. It's amazing what you can do with lots of public money and no need to make a profit.

Dad believed children had an obligation to visit their parents, so we frequently visited Grandmother Snee in Pleasant Hills. Grandfather Snee died in 1943. I remember going upstairs into a dark bedroom at Grandmother's house and seeing an old man in bed. He may have been quite ill and dying at the time.

Sunday family visits to the farm were commonplace when I was growing up. The discussions of farm business, family activities, politics, sports, etc. were all part of the spirited discussion centered around a wonderful meal. Farm families sure knew how to eat.

My Great-Grand Mother Davis also lived with Dad's mother. She was quite old and died at ninety-six or ninety-seven years of age. She was forgetful but wanted to have her purse hidden when company came. The purse contained all of five dollars that she never spent. Grandma Snee was a kind, gentle woman who loved all and was loved by all in return.

I fondly recall spending one or two weeks visiting her on separate occasions. I was younger than five at the time, I think, because I didn't wear glasses, and the grass looked "fuzzy" at her house. I remember the big oak tree out back and Uncle Tom's house up the Clairton Road about two or three lots away. At night I could see the red fire of the steel mill slag dump out the upstairs window. I'm reminded that Pleasant Hills is close to Pittsburgh, a steel town.

Grandma Snee was frugal and used tea bags at least two times, a habit of mine now. She also had a family recipe for an English pudding that was and remains a family Thanksgiving tradition. I wish my wife Marge made it more often.

It was common practice in those days to go visiting on Sundays. The Snee farm was a particularly nice place to visit: a different environment, good friends, food, and conversation. We got many visitors. Mom and Dad were very hospitable. Plus, that was the only way you could see them because they didn't go anywhere. They always were busy.

My cousin Karen Kreps DelGrosso offers her memories of visiting the Snee Farm:

> "Although I was young, probably 10 and younger, it was always such a treat to come calling at your house. Yes, in the summer we always brought our bathing suits, and sometimes we didn't, counting on a dip in the Ten Mile Creek. Wasn't there a rope swing you boys used to show off on when jumping into the water? I remember standing there wanting to do it too but was afraid. I always wanted to be a boy when we came to visit with you.
>
> "I also have great memories of visiting one time when you had hogs and someone—was it you or Tom?—showed off how I should ride the hogs. I learned quickly it was almost impossible. I'll bet your dad wouldn't have been too happy if he'd known we were riding the hogs.
>
> "I also recall Slick and how he barked and barked when we arrived and left in the car. The arrival wasn't too bad, but I always worried as Dad drove down the driveway rather quickly to get away from Slick that he'd drive the car off the edge. Strange, the things little kids worry about!
>
> "As I close my eyes, I can still see the inside of the barn, the rafters, and times when it was filled with hay. I thought it was great fun just jumping and rolling in the hay. I also have a clear memory of the inside of your house, the kitchen with the party line phone on the wall, the whole downstairs and the narrow

steps leading to the upstairs. The lawn in front of the house was always so perfect; I'm amazed at all the work you went to in accomplishing the results."

Some frequent visitors were Howard and Freda Salinger, Vie and Bill Arthur and girls, Jack and Sis Davis, Rolland and Shirley Snee and family, and Charlie Thatcher.

Freda Salinger had been Mom's friend since at least high school. She and her husband Howard introduced Mom and Dad to each other. They had two daughters, Bernice and Donna Mae, both of whom had responsible jobs in the steel mill, as did Howard. One of the byproducts of coming to the farm was a gift of horse manure for their roses and black walnuts they cracked and put in fudge. Howard also went hunting in the mountains with Dad.

Vie Arthur was another childhood friend of my mom's. She, Bill and daughters Mary Jo and Judy would come to the farm and stay a week for several years until the girls became teenagers. The first thing Bill did when they arrived was go to Rinky Dinks Bar—sometimes called the Midway—down the road and buy a case of beer. Mom and Dad didn't keep alcohol in the house. Vie had a very loud voice and often spoke before she thought. On one occasion at the county fair when walking through the beef barn, she spotted a large bull with an associated large set of testicles. She commented loudly and to my mother's great embarrassment, "My God, Helen! What a Man!" How right she was, as science has proven that a good predictor of the quality of a bull's progeny is the circumference of his scrotum.

There were many Vie stories. Another famous one had to do with a car accident. Vie was in the passenger seat of a car being driven by her sister. They came to a stop sign and Vie's sister asked, "How does it look down there?" Vie answered, "Fine." Her sister pulled out and was immediately hit by an oncoming car. Fortunately, no one was hurt badly. When her sister asked Vie why she had responded "Fine" when there was a car coming. Vie said, "You asked me how it looked. It was beautiful. It was fine. You didn't ask me if a car was coming."

Jack Davis was Dad's cousin on his mother's side. Jack was a doctor, as was his father, who was the attending physician at my birth and likely that of my two brothers as well. Mom and Dad helped Jack through school financially at W&J and University of Pittsburgh medical school. Jack was successful as a doctor and had an airplane that he used to fly over the farm on Sunday morning and drop a message saying they would come out to the farm in the afternoon. After a friend was killed in an airplane crash, Jack sold his plane.

Jack was also an avid crow hunter and would shoot as many as a hundred crows in a day. He knew where their flight lines were, and he would call them with an electronic crow call. We were always suspicious of Jack's kill count because we observed that he counted anything as a kill, even if all he saw was a feather drop or a sudden change in direction, commenting "I got him. He'll die later."

Jack was a character. While in school, he wrecked his car and sent his father the following telegram: "Saw shadow, thought it was a bridge, hit shadow, was bridge." His father wasn't amused.

Rolland T. Snee was Dad's son by his first marriage. He worked in the steel mill. He and his wife Shirley had two children, Becky and Terry. They used to make regular visits to the farm. Rolland T. liked to hunt groundhogs—among other varmints—and often did so when he and his family visited.

Charlie Thatcher grew up on a farm that was close to where my dad was born and raised. Charlie was several years younger than Dad and had great respect for my Grandfather Snee. Charlie would come to visit Dad on Sundays and talk up a storm. He had lots of good stories to tell about growing up on the farm that he shared with Dad, not always to his pleasure. Charlie made a lot of money from his car dealership and traveled a lot when he retired. Amazingly, he also went to Russia. Charlie had a keen interest in fine wood like oak and cherry and nut trees like walnut that he planted and nurtured on his farm in Somerset, PA. He was said to have a barn filled not with hay but fine furniture wood.

CHAPTER 10

ANIMAL HUSBANDRY

After the milk business was sold in 1950, Dad retired to the farm and Mom ran the ice cream business and dairy bar: an unfair deal. Mom did all the work and Dad had fun doing what he wanted and letting Mom pay the bills, which were many. I don't believe he ever had a year where he made money on the farm. But how did he know? Making money was not his objective. He never paid any attention to finances. His goal was to do whatever he wanted, regardless of the cost, a very selfish perspective, in my opinion.

My first recollection of the farm was the pig business, which started during the Korean War around 1950. Dad did it in a big way, having a herd size of around two hundred to two hundred fifty. We had pigs everywhere on thirty acres. Dad could sell them faster than he could raise them. Sometimes, he would sell them off the truck in Pittsburgh stockyards without ever going to the pens. The pigs would come off our truck, across the scales and into the buyer's truck.

Central to the farming business is the livestock auction. Two were in business when I was growing up and are still in operation today: Eighty Four auction in Eighty Four, PA held on Mondays, and the Waynesburg Auction in Waynesburg, PA held on Thursdays. Livestock of all sorts, mostly cattle, pigs and sheep, were sold mostly to slaughterhouses, but some animals found homes elsewhere. My dad consigned all types of livestock at these two auctions over the years. Farm dispersal auction sales were also held when farmers went out of business.

The central figure at an auction was the auctioneer. His job—all were men at the time—was to get the highest price for each animal. I found auctioneers to be very entertaining by their chant and bid taking routine. I guess my interest was in my blood, as my grandfather Charles E. Snee was a successful auctioneer in the Jefferson Township area near Pittsburgh. He had a farm there where my father and brothers and sister were born. The farm is now the Jefferson Memorial Cemetery in Pleasant Hills.

After hog prices went down, Dad got into the purebred Yorkshire pig business. Yorkshires are bacon hogs. He bought a five-hundred-pound boar that he named Duke from a farm in Indiana or Illinois, sight unseen. Duke arrived by rail. One or two females were also subsequently purchased in the same way. We showed the pigs at the county fair one or two years, but not much else happened with the pigs. Duke may have been Dad's favorite animal, as he was the only one I can remember him being photographed with.

Dad went out of the pig business when the pigs got a disease known as rhinitis, which stunted the growth of the pigs. The germ was in the soil and was difficult, if not impossible, to eliminate. It was suspected that

Dad and Duke, the purebred Yorkshire boar that dad purchased sight unseen from a breeder in the Midwest (Indiana or Illinois). Duke was large, weighing 400-500 pounds

the disease had come from the pigs we shipped in from the Midwest, but this was never confirmed. After the pigs came the Hereford beef cattle, commercial at first, and then the purebreds. That seemed to be Dad's way of acquiring and raising livestock.

Raising steers for slaughter presented an opportunity to create synergy with the dairy bar in town. The dairy bar was also a restaurant and sold bread among other things. The bakery that supplied the bread also made day-old bread and sweet rolls available to Dad. He took old bread and sweet rolls home and fed them to the cattle. How do you get cattle to eat bread? Very simple: Put them a pen and don't feed them anything else except bread and water. After short while, they ate the bread and even looked forward to it. After all, bread is made from wheat, a grain.

This was also an opportunity for my brothers, Duane Winnett and me. The sweet rolls, while a day old, still tasted good and were a treat. Duane would often come over for a sweet roll or two.

Several farms were involved in the beef cattle business in addition to ours: the Lacock farm down by Ten Mile—complete with a tenant farmer—and the Hallam place up past Mt Hermann Church. Dad's entry into the purebred business began with the purchase of a thousand-dollar horned Hereford bull at the annual Waynesburg purebred cattle sale consigned by his cousin Waldo Brown. Then there was the purchase of two purebred females, one of which was bred when purchased. The calf was Tom's 4-H project. The calf turned out to be a dwarf and was sent to auction, the place where all nonproductive animals ended up. The mother was bred to Dorsey Woodruff's prize bull and produced a decent bull calf. It won a few prizes at the fair, but I don't recall what happened to it.

Dad was always getting into some kind of trouble with his farm ventures and adventures, and it was no different with beef cattle. While hauling a load of cattle to new pasture he rented, Dad went around a corner too fast and upset a load of cattle in Washington near the area's hospital. A big roundup ensued, complete with the police wanting to shoot the cattle, which Dad opposed. The cattle were finally corralled in the Washington High School football field, loaded on a truck, probably Dorsey Woodruff's, and taken to the new pasture. This event made the local newspapers.

Next was the dairy cattle venture. This time, we were going to make money. The barns were below standard, and we could only sell the milk to Carnation Dairy, which sterilized the milk in the process of making canned milk. A new barn was planned but never built. Dad, of course, had Holstein cows that were good producers. Good dairy cattle were the result of artificial breeding, in which a female cow was medically inseminated by a veterinarian. That was the approach that Dad used. He never used artificial breeding with beef cattle, a popular practice today. He went out of the dairy cattle business by selling bred cows and heifers just before they were ready to calve. Dad probably made some money off this venture. Tom liked milking the cows, but I never did. I avoided it at every opportunity and would feed, water or clean up the manure, anything to get out of milking.

My brothers and I also got into the farming business in addition to 4-H projects. We would sell produce at a roadside stand that we would set up along Route 19 about a half-mile from the house. We sold tomatoes, cantaloupes and sweet corn among other things. In the fall, walnuts were a specialty. We would collect the walnuts and hickory nuts in our wagon by walking along the local dirt roads where the walnut and hickory trees were. There were no walnut trees on our farm. We would bring the walnuts home, shell them and let them dry in the sun for a few days. Shelling walnuts was an experience. The walnuts shells had a black stain that got all over our hands. We thought our stained hands were cool. After the walnuts had dried, we would sell them at our roadside stand. My brother Duane was a good salesman and always sold a lot of produce.

Throughout the years—whether it be pigs, beef cattle, sheep or dairy cows—animals would invariably get out and we would get a call from the neighbors to come get our animals. A few got hit by cars, including our pony, which had to be put down.

Fencing was always a problem, so Dad got another great idea. We would plant multi-flora rose bushes in the fence row. Over time a natural fence would develop because no animal would go through the resulting bolstered fence. After a few years, the idea worked well, but the plants kept on growing, often taking over good pasture. The only way to control the bushes, now weeds, was to spray them with brush killer. The solution to one problem had created yet another problem. And so it goes on a farm.

The animals had to be taken care of both morning and evening. The morning was a bit difficult. We were up at 6:00 a.m. with a wakeup call from my dad. My brothers and I each had our chores that had to be done before we caught the bus for school at 8:00 a.m. The chores were typically feeding and watering the animals. When we had dairy cows, they had to be milked. Milking was typically Tom's job. Everyone had a job; no excuses were tolerated.

Other than the disease that drove us out of the pig business, it wasn't clear why we moved from pigs to beef to dairy and finally to sheep. I believe it was a combination of not being able to make money at a venture and then becoming bored and not being fun anymore. Being the best or at least very good at whatever we did on the farm was always the goal. Clear evidence of this objective is all the county fairs at which we exhibited and competed, particularly with the sheep.

After raising pigs and beef cattle, Dad decided that the boys needed to be in the sheep business to stay busy. He bought fifty head of ewes at fifty dollars per head, a very high price for commercial sheep at the time. Snee Brothers were in the sheep business and twenty-five hundred dollars in debt. He also bought a ram and one purebred Hampshire ewe at the state sale in Harrisburg. The ewe was big and bred at the time of purchase.

I was around twelve years old at the time and Dad decided that I needed a 4-H project: two pens of four lambs to be raised and sold at the annual Western Pennsylvania 4-H Livestock Show and Sale at Herr's Island in the middle of the Allegheny River in Pittsburgh. The first year, my lambs placed third and fourth in the Hampshire division. The next year, my pen placed first in the same division. Then I hit it big: first Hampshire pen, Champion pen, Reserve Champion individual and winner of the fitting contest. The lambs sold for one hundred eighty dollars and the fitting contest prize was six dollars. The next two years, I had the Reserve Champion individual. I never won that illusive Champion Individual, which was where all the glory and the money were. The champion might sell for two dollars per pound and the reserve champion for ninety-five cents per pound. It was almost like coming in second in a gunfight. Everyone only remembers the winner, not who came in second.

One thing I was particularly proud of was the lambs we showed had been bred and raised on the Snee Farm. Our own creation! Almost all the other 4-H exhibiters purchased their lambs from various breeders.

Champion lambs. My 4-H projects included raising Fat Lambs that were shown and sold at the annual Western Pennsylvania 4-H Livestock Show and Sale held on Herr's Island in the middle of the Allegheny River in Pittsburgh. This picture shows my Reserve Champion Lamb in 1955.

Tom and Duane also had 4-H projects but never liked it as much as I did. It was fun and challenging and made me feel good about myself. The 4-H projects taught me several valuable lessons. The projects required me to keep financial records. I learned very quickly that what you made was a function of how much time you charged to your project and how much you made per hour.

Every project made money, as did my other projects on sheep breeding and growing potatoes. I raised Kennebec potatoes as a 4-H project for two years in the bottom field near Ten Mile Creek bordering the Youngman property. This location had sandy soil that was good for raising potatoes, enabling me to generate very high yields.

4-H also provided great growth opportunities. I experienced competition at county and state fairs and shows. I learned about winning and losing, although I was never a good loser. I'm better today but not good at it, much preferring to win. I learned the importance of keeping good records for both the performance of crops and animals, as well as the financial performance of the project. I learned how to value my time and see what return was derived from time spent completing projects.

Leadership is important, and I wanted to be president of the local 4-H club but was too bashful to pursue the office actively. I was vice president of the Amity 4-H club for one year. I had the desire to be a leader throughout high school and college but didn't achieve it until I got through graduate school and started my professional career.

It wasn't long before we added purebred Hampshire sheep to our commercial flock. We also started to show the sheep at the county fairs; over time we began to win regularly. This became a very big part of my life and to a lesser extent part of my brother's lives. It was a year-round endeavor. The ewes were bred in the summer and fall to lamb between

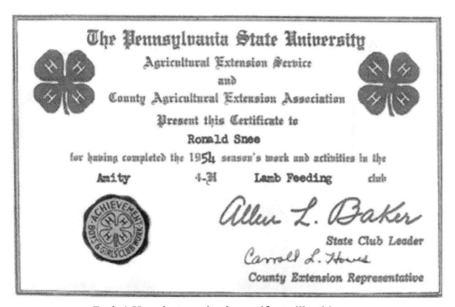

Each 4-H project received a certificate like this one,
which was for the fat lamb project

November and May. There were always problems with lambs and ewes dying at birth.

Ewes got pregnancy disease, which killed them if we didn't make sure they got lots of exercise. There we were every day in the winter, moving the flock around to keep the ewes alive until they had their lambs and all was well. We had no idea why exercise worked, but we did it because someone—I think the county agent—told us to do it. It was sad caring for animals all year and then losing them just when they were about to produce.

There were troubles throughout the year: fly maggots in the summer from urine-soaked wool, deaths due to stray dogs, foot rot, stud rams that didn't breed, and the loss of a whole year's crop of lambs. It sometimes seemed that sheep were born to die as quickly as possible. And it was always the good ones that died.

Over the years from 1954 until 1962 or so, we won many times at the county fairs and progressed to the point that we rarely lost. On successive weeks in August, we would show at the Jacktown—Wind Ridge—Greene County and Washington County fairs. Jacktown is the oldest, continuously operating fair in the country, having begun in 1885. Some years we would also go to Fayette County and Allegheny County. Once or twice, we competed at the Indiana County and West Alexander Fairs. In the good years, we would win a hundred dollars per fair. The standard routine was to bring the sheep to the fair on Sunday night and move them on to the next fair the following Saturday night.

The primary secret to our success was the breeding stock we added over the years. We purchased females from leading purebred breeders in Pennsylvania, Ohio, Virginia and elsewhere. The most important factor was our stud rams that were purchased at various times from Green Meadows Farms in Lancaster PA. At the time, this farm was arguably the premier breeder in the nation. We were honored that Ed Hess, one of the owners of Green Meadow Farms, attended our dispersal sale that was held in 1970. Thus ended an approximately twenty-year run of purebred Hampshire sheep on the Snee Farm.

Around 1960, I was appointed superintendent of the Wool Department at the Washington County Fair. This was not a big deal. On Show Day,

This Snee Brothers sign hung over the sheep pens in all venues. It was double-sided so passersby could see the sign no matter which direction they approached the sheep exhibit. Below the sign we hung the Purple (Champion and Reserve Champion), blue (first), red (second), white (third), etc., ribbons and banners our sheep had won.

the wool judge would rank the fleeces in various categories like fine wool and course wool. My job was to record the rankings in the fair records and pass out the ribbons: blue for first, red for second, white for third, and so on. Not a major responsibility. But it was nice to be given leadership responsibilities, even if ever so small.

When we were young, we would sleep at the fair in the back of Tommy Savage's or Buck Nichols' truck, in a vacant sheep pen, or in the hayloft above the sheep. The accommodations depended on the fair. Mom would give us a dollar a day for food. Hot dogs were $.15, hamburgers were $.25 and soft drinks were $.10. We would pick up a free meal on Show Day for helping Savage and Nichols show their sheep. We showed one breed: Hampshire. Nichols and Savage showed Hampshire, Southdown, Dorset, Cheviot and others, sometimes as many as fifty to sixty head compared to our twelve or so. They took home as much as four to five hundred dollars per fair. We were there to win. They were there for the money.

In addition to Buck Nichols and Tommy Savage, others who showed sheep at the fairs included Howard Shriver, a very successful Hampshire breeder; Santino (Junior) Barchessi; Benny Jacobs, who raised his Hampshire sheep in a chicken coop; Jimmy Caldwell; Sam Black; Charlie Orndorf, a popular auctioneer; and Charles M. Swart, a W&J graduate who showed Merinos, a fine wool breed of sheep. At Washington and Allegheny County fairs, we showed against Dr. Horace Gezon, a University of Pittsburgh professor who was known as a very formable competitor. Savage, Black, Barchessi, Jacobs and Caldwell pursued a career in farming. Buck Nichols worked a farm as well as teaching school. Buck ended up marrying Caldwell's sister.

I received an email from Buck sometime around 2000 and we corresponded frequently until his passing in 2019. In 2001 or 2002, I visited him as he was showing sheep at the West Alexander Fair. Leading his show flock at the time was a three-thousand-dollar Dorset ram he'd just purchased in Ohio. Some things don't change.

There was a great deal of work involved in showing sheep. They had to be washed with soap and water. We used a bathtub outside the back porch. Then, when dry, they were trimmed to look good for judging. We created special covers to keep the sheep clean until we showed them. Dad did most of the work in the beginning, but my brothers and I did it as we got older.

Example of the racks put on our pickup trucks to haul the sheep to shows and sales

In later years, the rules changed and required the sheep to be shorn, which reduced the amount of work we had to do to ready them for showing.

Showing the sheep at fairs and other expositions required hauling the sheep to and from the fairs. We had a lot of fun doing this and looked forward to the opportunity to be on our own. Every time Dad bought a new pickup truck, we had to build a new set of racks to haul the sheep. I helped Dad build one set. A few years later, he bought a new truck, and we needed a set for the new truck *in two days' time*. I went to town, bought lumber and bolts, and built the new racks. I created a new design: two stories. The top story was for the hay, straw, buckets, troughs, and other equipment. The racks were built out over the lowered tailgate. This extra room enabled the transport of an additional two to three sheep. The new racks worked very well. I was pleased and proud of my accomplishment.

I also built two sets of double gates for the barnyard that worked well and fit together well. Later in life, I would be criticized for not being a handyman. The truth is I completed lots of big construction jobs as a teenager.

One of a set of barnyard gates that I constructed to confine the sheep in the area of the barn

We also took sheep to sales, including annual events at Waynesburg, Indiana, Michigan State University, Harrisburg, Staunton, Virginia, and Carlisle. Many of these events were both shows and sales. The most prestigious were Staunton and Harrisburg. We usually stood near the bottom of the class at Staunton but on at least one occasion, we sold a ram privately at the sale. It was good experience and that was why Dad sent us there. I think Dad finally was able to sell at Staunton in the mid-sixties after I left the farm for Rutgers.

The first trip to Staunton, Virginia was very eventful. My directions from Dad were to take Route 19 south and take a left at Staunton. There were 250 miles in between. I was left to figure out the details on my own, which was usually the case with Dad. He did send my brother Duane along to help. We were seventeen and thirteen, respectively, at the time. I went to the service station at the top of Greene County hill and bought a map. We got there with no problems. I woke up the first morning in Staunton after sleeping in the sheep barn, and Duane and the truck were nowhere to be found! It turned out Duane had gotten up early and driven the truck to town for breakfast. When he showed up, he acted like everything was fine. Needless to say, I was scared out of my wits until he and the truck returned safely.

Champion ram at the Keystone Stud Ram Sale held in Harrisburg. This ram, shown here as a six-month-old lamb, sold for $365 as a yearling, a record price at the time.

One year we took a pair of ram lambs to Staunton; as usual,

we didn't make the cut. This turned out to be a blessing. We showed the pair at the fairs that summer and won several times. The following July, we took the best ram as a yearling to the Keystone Stud Ram Show and Sale at the Farm Show Building in Harrisburg. Our ram was champion of the Hampshire breed. We hit the big time! I also wanted the ram to sell well and not embarrass us. I thought two hundred dollars would be a good price.

In the sale ring, we quickly passed two hundred dollars, then three hundred, and I began to root for five hundred. I kept moving the ram around the ring and the bidding stopped at three hundred sixty-five dollars, a new record for the sale. Boy, was I excited and proud! They say that records are made to be broken and so was mine. A ram sold the following year for five hundred dollars. But I remained very proud of my accomplishment. When Dad sold the sheep in the late 1960's, the buyer came to our dispersal sale and told Dad what a great ram he was and that he was still using him. A very satisfied customer!

I got a very early lesson about biological variation from sheep. The following year, I sold a full brother to that same ram for sixty dollars, and that was what he was worth. Same mother and same father, with very different results.

Ram out of one of our stud rams purchased from Green Meadow Farms in Lancaster. This ram topped the Waynesburg Sheep Sale in 1962, selling for $100. He weighed 200-300 pounds as a yearling.

We learned many lessons from raising the sheep: the value of hard work, competition, winning and losing, making money, turning a profit, effects of variation, role of bloodlines and genetics, etc. It was a very satisfying part of my life that I look back on with great satisfaction.

Dad always had one or more dogs around, mostly as watchdogs for both humans and animals that didn't belong there. Two are most memorable: Slick and Joe. Slick was a small mongrel that showed up at the farm one day and never left. He was mostly white with a few black spots. Slick became the official guard dog. He let us know whenever anything foreign entered the farm property, humans and animals alike.

The origin of the name Slick goes back to the cowboy movies we saw frequently at the Wayne Theater. One of the cowboys in a movie we watched was called Slick. He was a small mean guy, always in trouble. Duane thought this matched our dog's behavior. So, he named the dog Slick and it stuck.

Slick was a good watchdog but also liked to chase cars and buses on Route 19 and the blacktop road that ran past the house. One day he got hit by a bus. After recovering, he walked on three legs for the rest of his life:

Hunting Dog Joe and Farm Guard Slick

two front and one rear leg. We could tell how cold it was by watching how high up Slick carried his rear leg. In the summer, it almost touched the ground. On cold days, he carried it about three inches above the ground.

Joe was a purebred brown and white German Pointer hunting dog. He was a good hunter and was trained by Dad to point grouse, quail and pheasants. Joe went on many hunts with us around the farm and in the mountains of Pennsylvania.

From time to time and after I left the farm, Dad would have dogs tied out by his garden to keep raccoons and groundhogs out of his vegetables. He didn't treat these dogs as well as Slick and Joe.

Dad hated cats and killed any he had an opportunity to kill. Mom liked cats and would have one or two around whenever possible. They would show up at our door, having been abandoned on the side of the road by someone—often from the city—to fend for themselves. One Sunday morning we got up and found one of Mom's cats dead under the pine tree. We immediately asked Dad what happened. He said he didn't know and suggested the cat must have had a heart attack. We didn't believe him, but that wasn't unusual, as he never admitted to anything. Another Amity mystery!

CHAPTER 11

HUNTING, FISHING AND TRAPPING

Dad was an avid hunter and hunted just about everything: grouse, quail, pheasants, rabbits, deer, ducks, geese, etc. He hunted in the mountains in Potter County and of course around home. An example of his view of hunting happened about one week after I was born, four days after the Japanese attacked Pearl Harbor. I was told by my mother that Dad suggested they buy me a gun. Dad was afraid guns would be rationed and he wouldn't be able to get me one at a later date. Mom had a different view of the situation and they eventually agreed there would be plenty of time for me to get a gun.

Dad never took us to the mountains except for one- or two-day trips to Juniata County to hunt grouse; we didn't get any on those occasions. When we were old enough to use them safely, he gave each of us a rifle and a shotgun.

In my teenage years, I took a liking to hunting squirrels and was successful. I liked the quiet solitude of sitting and enjoying nature. Dad and my brothers would traipse all over, looking for grouse and finding none. One day, I shot four squirrels, three grays and a fox squirrel, and they got nothing. I essentially quit hunting when I went to Rutgers in 1963. On one visit home, I went on a grouse hunt with Dad and the boys. As luck would have it, I shot a grouse in flight. Dad was more excited than I was. That's the only grouse I ever shot.

One day on a pheasant hunt, Dad admonished us not to shoot hens, which were not in season. After traipsing around all day and seeing nothing, we were tired and frustrated. We suddenly flushed out two hens We all got off one or two shots. Fortunately for the hen and us, we all missed. Of course, we all got a lecture from Dad about it. But it wasn't much of a lecture since he had shot as well.

After I went to Rutgers, Dad and my brothers became interested in deer hunting and were quite successful. I have yet to shoot a deer, but one year while I was in high school, Duane got to shooting doe out of season and I—as big brother—had to go out in the middle of the night and haul it home on foot through the woods.

Duane was a very determined hunter. One day he was squirrel hunting and tried to shoot a squirrel that would stick only its head out of a hole in a tree. Try as he might, he couldn't get the squirrel to leave the tree. In his impatience and frustration, he shot the squirrel in the head and then took a chain saw and cut the tree down to retrieve the squirrel. This all took place up in the hollow on the Bennett farm behind the barn. Our first knowledge of what happened was when Duane came down the hollow on the tractor dragging the log and holding the squirrel by the tail in his hand. Another successful hunt completed.

There were other kinds of hunting, including crow hunting with Jack Davis, Dad's cousin. Groundhogs were considered a varmint, as they would dig holes in the field that could cause injury to animals as well as damage to farm equipment. Groundhogs were hunted on our property and other properties as sport, often by cruising side roads and shooting out the car window. The way to get a good shot at a groundhog is to whistle and shoot the animal when it stood on its hind legs. Dad had a special rifle for hunting varmints: a 222 that shot a 22-caliber bullet. He called it his varmint rifle.

Skunk hunting was done differently. In the summer after the hay was cut, we would drive over the fields at night in the Jeep with the front window down and shoot skunks with the shotgun over the hood of the Jeep. My brothers and I were young at the time and Dad did the driving and shooting. It was great fun riding over the fields at night at fairly high rates of speed. We always looked forward to skunk hunts.

Living next to Ten Mile Creek made fishing a natural thing to do. We fished a lot and caught suckers, shiners, blue gills, sunfish, rock bass, bass—mostly small mouths—catfish and trout. We quickly learned that the best time to catch catfish was when the creek was high and muddy after a good rain. Catfish were the only fish to bite then. Catfish were fun to catch because they were big and put up a fight. Most of the fish we caught were five to ten inches long. Catfish were often fifteen to twenty inches. Once a year, Mom would take us to Grimm's Lake to fish for catfish and carp. We looked forward to the outing and often caught some big ones. We ate many of the fish we caught. Dad wasn't much of a fisherman and rarely took us fishing.

Of course, trout were the prize. The creek was stocked each year and we would all go fishing the first day of trout season. This was the in thing to do. Hackney's bottom was a favorite place to go, and we caught our share. Tom and Duane were particularly good at catching trout and other fish, for that matter. Tom, and Duane to a lesser extent, became avid trout fishermen. It was not unusual for them to fish up and down the Ten Mile Creek for trout and, on occasion, bass. Tom is a good fly fisherman and has passed the skill along to his sons.

We also trapped along the creek, catching raccoons, muskrats, mink and opossums at one time or another. Dad would take the unskinned animals to town and sell them to George Bedillion. Typical prices were a dollar for opossum, three to four dollars for muskrats, five dollars for raccoons and ten to twenty dollars for mink. Bedillion had a stock comment anytime we brought furs in for him to sell: "Furs aren't bringing much these days." As you might expect, Bedillion's place had a foul smell, to say the least, with so many dead animals to be skinned.

At one point, we decided we would skin the animals, stretch the hides, and sell the pelts to some fur house at higher prices. This turned out to be a nuisance. I don't remember the details but suffice it to say we quickly went back to selling the unskinned animals to Bedillion. The higher prices weren't worth the time and effort required to get the pelts ready for sale. Besides, the fun was in trapping the animals, not selling the pelts, although the money was nice.

As you might expect we caught few minks, less than five as I recall. Tom had the best luck; he may have caught all five! Johnny Golsky was really good at catching mink, but he would never tell us his secret. I guess he wanted the mink for himself. At my mother's direction, we put the money we earned—usually split three ways—in the bank.

Dad taught us how and where to set the traps. Each morning before school, in addition to feeding the animals, we would check to see if we caught anything. We knew that warm rainy nights were the best because on very cold nights, the animals didn't run. As we got older, the prices decreased to next to nothing and we moved on to other things.

CHAPTER 12

SPRING AND SUMMER

We had about two acres of lawn around the house. I enjoyed cutting the lawn and took over the duties. For many years, we used a self-propelled golf course mower. In later years, we used the tractor with a rotary bush hog mower on the back. It was satisfying to complete the mowing and keep the lawn looking nice. We often got behind and the grass clippings had to be raked. This was a big job because it was done by hand.

I also enjoyed the solitude of mowing. No one bothered me. I was able to think and let my mind wander. I still enjoy mowing the lawn today.

At one time or another, beginning in our early teens, my brothers and I operated each piece of farm machinery and were very proud of our skills. Dad thought safety was important and early on stressed the safe way to operate each piece of equipment. I enjoyed plowing the ground in the spring and planting corn and other crops. I was particularly pleased when all the corn rows came out straight. I would often work until 9:00 or 10:00 p.m. Like mowing the lawn, there was solitude, and I could get lost in my thoughts. It was often a very peaceful time for me.

After the work on the farm was done, we made time for play. *We created our own entertainment.* There was a foursome involved: Duane Winnett, me and my two younger brothers, Tom and Duane. We were close in age, with

Duane Winnett and one of several ponies he rode to the Snee Farm. *Left to right:* Duane's Pony, Duane Winnett, Ronnie Snee, Louise Williams (my mother's sister), Tommy Snee, Duane Snee and Helene Snee (my mother)

Mom, Dad and the boys (circa 1955)

four years between us. Duane Winnett was the oldest; my brother Duane was the youngest. Ten Mile Creek was the center of a lot of the activity.

Our first introduction to the creek was at the riffles just below the house, within twenty yards of the driveway. The water was shallow above the riffles and good for wading. We often fished below the riffles. The riffles were the result of the remains of an old grist mill. My brother Tom's research in later years found that these remains were from the Swartz Mill that was built around 1786. In colonial days, there were grist mills all along the streams in Western Pennsylvania, often being some seven to eight miles apart. This was necessary, as travel was difficult in those days and people couldn't travel far regularly to get their grain milled.

The grist mills were important economically for grinding wheat and corn for both human and animal consumption. It cost a lot of money to transport grain to market along the Route 40 Trail back to Cumberland, Maryland, and points east. The farmers got the idea to grind their grain (hence the need for grist mills), use it to make whiskey and then ship the whiskey east for sale, an easier and more profitable endeavor than selling grain.

In the 1790's, George Washington was president and Alexander Hamilton was treasurer of the United States. Our young country needed money to operate, and under Hamilton's leadership, a tax was levied on whiskey and other spirits. This greatly affected the western Pennsylvania economy, resulting in the Whiskey Rebellion (1791-94), which quickly ended when Washington led the military in to enforce the laws. The farmers thought better of their rebellious idea: Washington had given them a lesson in clear thinking. The suppression of the Whiskey Rebellion was the first, and only time an American president, as Commander in Chief, had led the us armed forces into the field and established federal authority over the states.

During the summer we swam in Ten Mile Creek. We never had swimming lessons. We just jumped in the water and taught ourselves. This was an important skill to learn, as we often fell in the creek when we were fishing. Our favorite place to swim was the Gypsy Camp, a swimming hole in Ten Mile Creek on the southwestern edge of the Snee Farm, about four hundred yards from the house. It was great to take a swim during the summer after a hard day's work. People came from all over to swim there. The origin of the term Gypsy Camp is unknown to me. Very few, if any, spent the night there.

The problem we encountered almost every year was the lack of a diving board. My brothers, Duane Winnett and I would have to build a diving board so we could dive into the stream. Over the winter floods would erode the bank around the diving board and we would have to replace it each summer. This wasn't a big deal. We would get a two inch by twelve or sixteen inch board that was twelve to sixteen feet long. We would dig a hole in the creek bank and then place a big stone on the edge of the bank under the board to give it some bounce. Next, several big rocks were placed on the end of the board that was in the creek bank. The dirt was then filled in and tamped. The arrangement of the board and the stones created a fulcrum that gave spring to the board. Sometimes our construction needed repair and a redo or two, but we always got the job done. We had a diving board that lasted all summer and sometimes the following year if the floods weren't too bad.

Duane Winnett often came over to go swimming. Duane was often the source of the actual board for our diving board. His dad, Wally, owned a lumber mill. We also went swimming in the dam on his grandfather's farm. Once a year, Mom would take us swimming for a day at Sunset Beach on Route 40 west of Washington. We also often went there with church groups. Dad never participated in our swimming activities but never discouraged them either. Swimming in Ten Mile Creek was also popular when relatives and friends came to visit.

We also camped along Ten Mile Creek across from the Gypsy Camp. The McAfee brothers—Harvey, Bill (Brownie) and Ronnie and others—were frequent campers. We slept in Army tents and cooked our meals, pancakes, fish, etc., over a wood fire. Fishing, swimming, and building rafts were popular activities. Sometimes we would cut down trees with axes and saws and then float the trees down the creek to a selected point, where we would build a raft. The campsite was on the Snee Farm, so we were not far from home.

CHAPTER 13

FALL AND WINTER

We celebrated all the holidays in the appropriate way, but Halloween was has special memories for me because we could go out and be little devils after dark. At first, we dressed up and went trick or treating, which included soaping cars and house windows in Amity. As we got older, we began playing pranks on people. On several occasions, we would stretch toilet paper across Route 19 and delight in cars and trucks coming to a screeching halt to avoid driving through the toilet paper. We also threw stones on Louie Jenkins' roof and rolled his rain barrel down the red dog road beside his house. This made a very loud noise and angered Louie to the point that he would fire his shotgun in the air to scare us off. To us, that meant we won the game.

Red dog was used to pave the dirt roads in western Pennsylvania. It was in abundant supply as a result of the waste from the coal mines. The slag and other waste were removed from the mines and put in a big pile that would catch fire due to spontaneous combustion. The pile was huge and burned for years. The resulting smoke and fumes killed all the vegetation in the immediate area. The result was red dog, a hard, red stone substance. When the fire cooled down, the township road crew would load the red dog on dump trucks and use it to pave and repair the township roads. Hence, the term red dog roads.

My brothers, Duane Winnett and I really got in trouble one year on Halloween when we barricaded the road by Hackney's bottom with corn shocks. It was fun to watch people stop, get out of their cars, and move the corn shocks so they could continue their journey. It worked like a charm, and we stopped several cars. When we returned home, a two-mile hike through fields and woods, there was the constable was waiting on us. We quickly confessed and Dad paid Hackney for the damaged corn. Dad wasn't too hard on us, as he understood what had happened. That was one of the things you did on Halloween in the county, but we never figured out how the constable got onto us so quickly.

In the winter, snow would fall, sometimes in large amounts, and sled riding became a popular activity. We would go sled riding down the lane to our house. But the good sledding was on the Winnett farm, which had steep, long hills. When the sledding was good, many kids of all ages would go to the Winnetts, mostly in the moonlight. We rode a variety of sleds: regular two-runner sleds, one-runner Yankee Jumpers, shovels and even pieces of roofing tin.

We got the idea to make a twelve- by three-foot piece of roofing tin into a bobsled by turning up one end and connecting some bailing wire to the two front corners to form a handle to guide the front. We would then seat ourselves, with Tom in front to guide the bobsled. Duane, Ron and Duane Winnett brought up the rear. We rode the bobsled on the steep hill far behind the Winnett's house, which was more than three or four hundred feet long. The sled traveled at a very high speed like an unguided missile. Also, there were no brakes. To stop, we simply rolled off at the bottom of the hill to keep from ending up in the stream at the foot of the hill. It was an exciting, dangerous, and fast trip down the hill. It's a wonder no one got hurt.

There was one occasion not to be forgotten. On one ride down the hill, Tom forgot to roll off the bobsled and ended up in the frozen stream, falling partially through the ice. We fished him out, took him to the Winnett house, warmed him up and gave him some of Opal's famous chili. All was well. We took a break from bobsled riding for the rest of the day. The sledding stopped when we became teenagers; it wasn't cool anymore.

Spring Flood. Ten Mile Creek froze over during very cold winters. Heavy spring rains would break up the ice. The water would pour into our bottom field.

Ten Mile Creek would freeze over in the winter, and we would skate up and down the creek, play hockey and fox and geese on the ice. This was often a night activity with a big fire, fueled by a tire, to provide light and heat. Duane Winnett was a frequent participant in such events.

The ice didn't last forever. As spring arrived, heavy rains would raise the water level, and the ice would break up into large chunks of ice, sometimes eight to ten inches thick, lying in the creek bed. Flood water would pour into our lower fields. This was repeated all along Ten Mile Creek. The flood deposited debris of all types in the fields along the creek, wiping out fences and causing other damage.

From time to time, we had huge snowstorms. Two are most memorable. On Thanksgiving of 1950, it began to snow. It continued for two or three days, leaving two to three feet of snow on the ground. We were snowed in and couldn't get out for almost a week. Dad built a plow on the front of the Jeep and pushed his way to the main road, which had been plowed. Our dog Slick rode in the Jeep as Dad plowed his way out. It was work for Dad but fun for my brothers and me; we got to go sled riding.

Large chunks of ice would lie in the creek bed. This was repeated all along Ten Mile Creek. The flood deposited debris of all types in the fields along the creek, wiping out fences and causing other damage.

Don Dunbar, husband of my cousin Edith Snee Dunbar, told me, "Your Dad's ability to rig a snowplow for the front of the Jeep in November of 1950 wasn't a surprise to me. Those Snee boys (my dad Rolland and his brothers, my uncles Duane, Tom and Charles) could always improvise." I was to learn later in life how talented the Snee boys (my uncles) were.

On some occasions, the Winnetts would come over and plow out our driveway for us. In later years, my dad purchased a plow for the tractor, and it was much easier and quicker to manage snowstorms.

Sometime around 1961, I was coming home from Washington via Route 19 South in the Nash Rambler with no snow tires. I was doing a great job of driving up the hills and got almost to Amity when a truck stopped in front of me and I got stuck just above Willis Ramsey's house. I could barely see five feet in front of me. I walked in a blinding snowstorm to the Ramsey house, arriving completely covered with snow. I was welcomed, of course. I called home and someone came to get me.

A day or two later after the roads had been plowed, I went to get the car. It was in a snowbank completely covered by the snow from the plows. Tom or Duane and I dug the car out and towed it home. Close to home we started it in gear, warmed it up for a while and all was well. Another adventure ended. The interesting thing is I only needed to go another hundred yards or so above the Ramsey residence and it would have been all downhill to home. I could have gotten home just fine if only that truck hadn't gotten stuck in front of me!

CHAPTER 14

BASEBALL WITH SAM COOPER AND MR. BRISTOR

When Duane was nine and Tom was eleven, a little league team was started by Art Bristor's dad and others. Tom played infield, catcher, and pitcher. Duane played second base, shortstop, and pitcher. They were both good players and played on several little league and pony league all-star teams. I went to the games but couldn't play because I was too old.

The Amity team had some success but had trouble with the river teams like Millsboro. Many of their players were big and strong and could really hit the ball. As the Amity players got older, they started a pony league and combined with Lone Pine and other teams. These teams were managed by Sam Cooper, whose son Fred played. On one occasion when the team was getting badly outscored, Sam told his son Fred—who was pitching—to throw it down the middle and see how far he could hit. Rumor has it that he hit it a fair distance! Sam was a schoolteacher and one of the original Pittsburgh Steelers. Fred became a good football player and later played quarterback at the University of Maryland.

Johnny Golsky, a coal miner, hunter, and trapper, liked Tom and Duane and taught them how to pitch. Johnny had been a good sandlot player in his day. I remember Amity's sandlot teams playing on the ball field in Winnett's bottom. Winnett's dog Blacky was trained to retrieve balls that were hit into Ten Mile Creek. Blacky was a long-haired, part collie. Each spring Blacky would get sheared when the sheep got sheared. During sandlot baseball games, we would wait for a ball to land in the creek. We would throw a stone or stick near the ball to show Blacky where the ball was, and he would swim out and get it. As a result, we'd have a newfound treasure: another baseball .

I recall seeing the Amity sandlot team playing the Homestead Grays at least once. It wasn't until later in life that I recognized what a great piece of history I had witnessed. The Homestead Grays team was a big deal in the Negro leagues and had many famous players. Homestead, which was near Pittsburgh, is where my mother was born and raised.

For as long as I can remember, Wally Winnett let ball teams use his field. The field had to be kept neat, clean and mowed. Games were not allowed on Sundays, as the crowd noise disturbed Wally's afternoon nap. The field is now called the Amwell Township Ballpark.

Golsky taught Duane how to throw a sinker and Duane got pretty good with it. In a game with a group of Washington all-stars, Duane struck out Bob Reigel, Bob Stock and Ted Vactor, three outstanding athletes, in a row. They were embarrassed to be struck out by a farm kid. They all played NCAA Division I football and Vactor played in the NFL for Atlanta. Duane was very proud of that accomplishment and to this day delights in telling the story.

I was too old to play baseball in the little league and pony league with Tom and Duane, but I regularly went to their games and was an avid fan. Trinity High ran a summer program under the direction of Milt Decker for the five townships that sent kids to Trinity. I was asked to play and did so for one season. On the team were Craig Walters, Orville Richmond, Clifford Hupp, Ronnie McAfee and others. They were all younger than me, but since I was born in December, I was allowed to play. I played first base. They wanted me to pitch because I was left-handed, but Mr. Decker said I was too old. I had a good year. I hit better than 300, with a whole bunch of singles and one triple that I hit in a game on the Amity ball field at Winnetts. Our team made the playoffs but lost in the finals.

One play I can still see in my mind after more than fifty years was during the semifinal game that we were not supposed to win. I was playing first base. After a putout at first base, the runner at second took off for third. I threw the ball as hard as I could to our third baseman, Ronnie McAfee. It was a poor throw, but Ronnie somehow caught it. As the runner went by, Ronnie whirled around and tagged him out, ending the game and sending our team to the championship game.

My only other experience at playing organized ball was a few softball games at the Lone Pine field. The rest of the guys were very big and could hit the ball a mile. I was very good at hitting singles by hitting the ball where there were no fielders. I would get a hit four out of five times, which frustrated the opposing team. Many years later, I played first base for a softball team in Manasquan, New Jersey, when I would go to the Jersey shore to visit my wife's family during the summer. I could still hit well.

CHAPTER 15

LESSONS IN BIOLOGY – FLORA AND FAUNA

Living and working on the farm was a great lesson in biology. We learned about the birds and the bees very early! We saw pigs, sheep and cattle mate, followed them through the gestation period, often witnessed the subsequent births and on occasion had to help the mothers deliver their young when they were having trouble with the birthing process. Some young animals had to be helped through the birth canal. Some died at birth, both mother and newborn. Our animals grew up to be sold for meat or breeding stock and were sometimes put in a herd as replacements.

We also learned about wild animals through hunting pheasants, quail, rabbits and squirrels; trapping raccoons, muskrats, minks and opossums; fishing for trout, bass and catfish; and by just watching.

Although we didn't recognize it at the time, we became aware of biological variation early in life. We observed two animals mated one year that produced outstanding offspring. The next year the same two animals might produce very common offspring. We saw corn and grain yields vary in different parts of the field due to variations in soil moisture or soil fertility. Some tomatoes grown on the same plant at the same time were bigger than others. There was no end to the amount and magnitude of variation we witnessed and sometimes felt.

On one occasion we got a lesson in a common cow and sheep disease, *bloat,* which happens when an animal eats too much fresh clover or alfalfa. The overeating of the lush grass produces stomach gas that blows the animal up like a balloon and will cause death if not treated. As luck would have it, Dad's prize milk cow, Ruby, got out into the alfalfa field.

When Dad found Ruby, she was about to die. Dad instantly pulled out his penknife and stuck her in the correct place in the correct stomach—not an easy feat, as cows have four stomachs—to relieve the pressure. Dad inserted a plastic tube in the hole, which continued to whistle for at least twelve hours. Ruby recovered and was a good milk producer for many years to come. From time to time, Dad had to perform other procedures on the animals. He had a good success rate, but not all survived.

We also learned the names of all the farm crops, trees, and grasses. One seventh or eighth grade project was to bring samples of wood from five to ten trees to school. I must have brought in samples of at least twenty trees. I probably could have found even more.

Dad taught us much about farm and wildlife biology. He enjoyed teaching us about all things agriculture. I still make frequent use of that learning today, as much of my work over the years has involved biological systems. I've never had a formal course in biology, but I've published several research papers in biology journals.

In my graduate work and faculty assignment at Rutgers University, I worked with the following departments: animal science, horticulture, entomology, plant pathology, food science and meteorology. In each of these departments, I encountered problems I had seen in one form or another growing up on the farm.

CHAPTER 16

TRINITY HIGH SCHOOL 1955-1959

Going to Trinity High School (THS) meant getting up early, feeding the animals, eating breakfast, and riding the school bus fifteen miles to town. As usual, I wanted to do well. I got a C in algebra the first marking period and decided I needed to work harder. I got mostly As after that. I made good grades overall, and although I had trouble with English, I finished fifteenth out of approximately two hundred fifty students in my senior class. I felt pretty good about that. In 2023 I received the Distinguished Trinity High School Alumni Award.

One experience I remember well was in study hall before classes started in the morning. On days when we would have tests scheduled, the brains of the class—John Yauch, Sandy Pinsker, Don Worth and Dick Scott—would study together during study hall. They had gone through grade school together and knew each other well. They didn't invite me to participate, so I would sit behind them and listen. My theory was that they knew the answers and what else was important to know. This developed into a very effective strategy for me. Bottom line: Listen to others when the opportunity presents itself.

Although the faculty at THS was not a stellar group, there were a few that I remember today. Mathematics was perhaps the best department, with Mrs. Mary Mansbarger teaching plane geometry to sophomores and

Mr. Joseph Smith teaching trigonometry and solid geometry to seniors. I got Mr. Smith to teach us how to use a slide rule on his lunch break. My cousin Teddy Weber was an engineering student at Pitt and got me a slide rule. I wanted to get a jump on college and learning to use the slide rule would help.

Another good teacher was Mr. Stanley Dubelle, who taught civics, part of which was Pennsylvania history. To encourage us to keep up with the news, he put an extra credit current events question on all tests. All we had to do was watch the evening news on television—yes, we did have television in the country—and we had the answer to the extra credit question. I credit that exercise with helping me develop the habit of watching the evening news. Mr. Dubelle was also a very fine wrestling coach. He taught wrestling in large part just like he taught any other course: Be organized and thorough, focus on the fundamentals and use repetition.

Mrs. Margaret Wylie taught us that seeing is not observing. It was a very simple demonstration. We had been in her English class for several months when she asked us to tell her what the design in the border around the ceiling of the room was. No one could answer the question. It was very embarrassing, an experience I still recall to this day.

And then there was Latin class. The textbook was full of quotations we had to learn. I recall two phrases: Experientia Docet—experience is the best teacher—and Tempus Fugit—time flies. I also recall two other things from the book. On one page someone had written, "For something shocking, turn to page 99." I quickly turned to page 99 to find written the word "electricity." I'd been had!! I suspect I was not the first person to fall for it. In another place, I found the unforgettable musing:

"Latin is a dead language, dead as it can be.

First it killed the Romans and now it is killing me!"

I didn't participate in any sports until my junior year when I went out for wrestling. Wrestling was a big deal at Trinity High. My brother Tom wanted to go out for the team. Tom got to do what he wanted and talked

Dad into saying yes. Dad couldn't say no to me, so I also got to go out for the sport.

I worked hard and learned a lot but never made varsity. I did wrestle two junior varsity matches with a 1-1 record. I wasn't given much of a chance by the coach, Stanley DuBelle. He wanted to create champions and I started too late in his view. Trinity High produced several state champions and at least two NCAA champions.

It was frustrating, but I set my goal on learning enough to wrestle in college, which I did. I had a successful wrestling career at W&J and had a great time doing it. Wrestling was a great learning and growing experience for me. Tom and Duane both made the team and were very successful. They both won Section Championships and received wrestling scholarships to Lycoming College.

High school was also a social maturing process for me that continued through college and all through life.

CHAPTER 17

COLLEGE YEARS 1959-1963

Going to college meant going to Washington and Jefferson College (W&J). My parents told me it was a good school, that eleven of my relatives went there and that was what they would pay for. I visited Kenyon College in Ohio, but it didn't interest me. I wanted to wrestle to prove I could do it successfully, since I hadn't made the team at Trinity. W&J had a team. I was awarded a half-tuition scholarship.

In September of 1959, I enrolled in W&J, majoring in three-two engineering: three years at W&J and then two years at Carnegie Tech, to get bachelor's degrees from both schools. In the first semester, I got a D in economics and was told to switch my major. Math was suggested. I agreed and that was the end of my engineering career. I never looked back. I liked math and this decision set a pattern for years to come. I focused my career on those things I enjoyed doing. Today, I see myself as a statistical engineer, solving important problems in several arenas using statistical thinking and methods.

Several of my high school classmates also went to W&J: John Yauch (MD), Dave Bryant (MD), Sandy Pinsker (Ph.D., English), Bob Ellenberger (Business Executive) and Chuck Dunn, who left W&J after one year. I stayed in contact with John over the years and see Dave, Bob and Sandy at high school and college reunions.

I struggled with English, philosophy, religion and other liberal arts courses but nailed math and science. I improved every year and made the Dean's list both semesters of my senior year. I graduated with a 3.0 GPA overall, a 3.6 in math and forty-ninth in a class of 149. Wray Brady—head of the Math Department—recommended me to Ellis Ott, Head of Rutgers' Statistics Center: "Snee is not the brightest student we have, but he is not the dumbest one either." It worked, as I got an assistantship at Rutgers worth $2200 a year, plus tuition to graduate school. Once again, I was very fortunate, as I was to learn that Dr. Ott and Dr. Brady had a lot in common. They could understand one another even at a distance over the phone.

When I applied to graduate schools I applied only to those schools that didn't have an application fee. I was a poor student and didn't have the money. I did make an exception. My wrestling coach, John Andrews, had coached football at Rutgers University and told me that it was a good school. I wanted to study statistics and Rutgers had a statistics program, I decided to apply to Rutgers but I didn't send along my $10 application fee.

An interesting exchange of letters had occurred between me and Rutgers from the time I applied and the time I sent my acceptance letter. In brief, Rutgers' responses to my letters went as follows:

> "Dear Mr. Snee, Thank you for your application. Please send a transcript of your grades and the $10 application fee"

> "Dear Mr. Snee, Thank you for sending your transcript. Could you have two professors write letters of recommendation for you, and also please send in your $10 application fee?"

> "Dear Mr. Snee, We have received letters of recommendation from Drs. Brady and Mansfield. Could you also please send us your $10 application fee"?

And so it went. I finally sent in my $10 application fee along with my letter of acceptance. One must be frugal when you don't have a lot of money.

Dr. Brady was an interesting character. He lived in the country between Amity and Washington off Route 19 near Dan Day Hill. He was a W&J

alumnus. He used blackboard work a lot: "Let's go to the boards" was his forte, sending all the class to the blackboard around the room to answer the questions he posed. I often felt it was a way to use up time when he didn't have anything else planned for the day.

He was the most applications-orientated instructor I had at W&J. He taught me the first application of mathematics. The problem was to decide when to sell a calf. Exercise 9 on page 89 of the *Calculus* book by Wray Brady and Maynard Mansfield states:

"A calf weighs 300 pounds and is gaining weight at the rate of one pound per day (you may assume that the weight of the calf increases continuously). Calves are selling at 35 cents per pound, but the price is falling at the rate of one cent per month (you may assume that the price decreases continuously). How many days hence should the calf be sold to realize a maximum profit? (For the purposes of this problem, one month lasts 30 days.)."

The value of the calf rose and fell as described by a quadratic curve. The curve passes through a maximum when the first derivative equals zero. This was neat! I knew what he was talking about, and his model was correct. For those interested, the time to sell is 375 days hence.

Dr. Brady thought well enough of my abilities to recruit me as an instructor on two occasions: at W&J and later at the University of Bridgeport in Connecticut. I was flattered but turned down both offers. I was in graduate school at the time and promised myself that I would not leave graduate school until I either got my PhD or they told me that wouldn't award it to me.

W&J gave me my first experience as a commuter. My deal with Dad was that I would work for him in the ice cream business, and he would give me a ride to school and pay my tuition. It was clear in the first week that being on time was not in Dad's paradigm. I hated being late, but Dad appeared not to care. I decided to hitchhike to school fifteen miles each way and did so for almost all my freshman year. I never missed a day of school. I was never late for class, several of which met at 8:00am.. I always felt that Dad didn't hold up his part of the deal. In April I decided to get a job and got one at the Washington Motel as a room clerk at one dollar per hour. Dad agreed to let me drive the pickup truck to school if I bought the gas, which I did. I saved my earnings for school. I paid for all my school expenses after the first year.

Hitchhiking turned out to be not such a big deal. I found regular rides. People liked helping the college boy. The days were long. In the winter, I left before dawn and returned after dark. I got it down to a science. When I had a class at the south end of campus, I would catch a ride with one person. If I needed to be at the north end of campus, I would get on the road at a different time and catch a ride with a different person, who would drop me off at the north end of campus.

Picture of me after winning the Presidents Athletic Conference 147# Wrestling Championship in 1963 held at Allegheny College in Meadville

I wanted to make the wrestling team because I had something to prove. It was a struggle my freshman year, but I made the team and wrestled in every match W&J had during my four years there. My records were 5-2-1, 7-3, 11-1, 12-0 for a composite 35-6-1. In my senior year, I was undefeated, conference champion at 147 pounds, elected team captain and selected as the outstanding wrestler of the 1962-63 season. I was satisfied and retired from competitive wrestling, although I remained a lifelong fan of the sport. I owe much to the experience and was honored to be elected to W&J's Athletic Hall of Fame in 2015.

During my first two years, Ed Chupa was the coach. He never wrestled and didn't know the sport. He was a disaster as a coach. In my last two years, John Andrews was the coach. He didn't know wrestling either, but he knew how to coach and was a quick learner. He at least got us into shape. It was during my junior year,

1961-62, with Andrews as our coach that the team won the President's Athletic Conference (PAC) Wrestling Championship. This was the first PAC Championship won by any W&J athletic team. We placed second my senior year, losing by only two points. These were pioneering years for wrestling at W&J, which had restarted the sport in 1959 after abandoning it in the early 1950's. Andrews later suggested I apply to Rutgers graduate school, one of the best decisions I ever made.

At W&J, I had to learn wrestling on my own, as did the other team members. Every chance I got, I went to Trinity and Washington High to work out and learn. They had great coaches who knew the sport and produced Pennsylvania state champions, Stan Dubelle—Trinity and Stan Mousitis—Washington High, who were related by marriage.

Some matches stick out in my mind. The first two matches I wrestled as a freshman were at 167 pounds. I wasn't strong enough at that weight and lost one and tied one out of two matches. In the first match at Muskingum in Ohio, I was winning with fifteen seconds to go in the third period and got taken down for a tie because I was out of shape and too tired. I made a vow never to be out of shape again and I never was. I got great pride out of seeing my opponent tired. I rarely, if ever, lost a match in the third period after that.

In my junior year, I lost only one regular season meet: to Dave Haley from Case Western Reserve. He beat me 16-14 in the highest scoring match of my career. At the end of the second period, with the score at 10-9, referee Doc Harris thought the match was over because of the high score. We still had another period to go. I wrestled Haley in the conference tournament later that year and he beat me 6-4. I had a bad knee at the time, which affected my confidence. I have a great appreciation today for athletes who participate with injuries. Haley was the only wrestler to beat me twice.

There was a wrestler, John Bernhard from Allegheny College, who won the President's Athletic (PAC) Conference championship four times. I wrestled him twice in the regular season in my sophomore and senior years and beat him easily both times, 6-4 and 1-0. In my senior year, he moved up to 157 pounds for the tournament to avoid me and defeated our Frank

Mika in the finals. If Mika had won, we would have won the title and been conference champs again, having won the title the previous year in 1962. Of course, if a couple of other close matches had gone our way, we would have won the championship, so we couldn't really lay it at Mika's feet. Our wrestling team had the honor of being the first W&J team to win a PAC championship. The golf team also won a PAC championship later in the spring of 1962. Both teams were coached by John Andrews.

Perhaps my best match was my last match in the finals of the PAC Championships. I wrestled Ken Narducci, a good wrestler from Thiel College. Jimmy Pareso had lost to him earlier in the year. I had a bye in the first round and pinned my opponent from Wayne State in the second round. In the finals, my opponent, Ken Narducci and I were tied 0-0 near the end of the first period and he got my right leg in the air and was about to get the advantage. There was only one move open to me, a single arm drag. This was a move I had practiced many times but never used in a match. I shot the move and it worked. I scored two points and rode him out for the rest of the period.

I had the choice in the second period and took bottom. Halfway through the period, I escaped and had a 3-0 advantage, which I maintained at the end of the period. I rode him for the entire third period and got an additional one point for riding time advantage, winning the match 4-0. Anytime you shut out your opponent, you've done a great job. I was very proud of my performance, and still am today. A near perfect performance was a great way to end a career!!

Wrestling was also a growth experience for me. Being an introvert, it's a big deal to get up in front of a group. In a wrestling match, it's me and my opponent in front of the crowd. I always wanted to do well, and my opponent was always out to make me look as bad as possible. Being successful in this arena helped me build self-confidence.

Wrestling at W&J produced several lifelong friends: John Yauch, Jim Pareso, George Zannos, Bill Ruha, Ken Getty and Lou Pogoreltz. We've stayed in touch over the years and frequently get together at W&J functions and wrestling matches, including the NCAA Division I National Championships.

Careful preparation was put into preparing for each wrestling match. This included practice during the week, discussion of what your opponent might do and psychological preparation on match day. The more focused and prepared we were, the better the results. I carried this habit and skills over into later life, particularly in dealing with senior management, where I view every meeting like a wrestling match to be planned and prepared for, with as little as possible left to chance. Just as with wrestling, when I'm prepared for a meeting with senior management, it usually goes well. I win the match and get what I need.

This experience came back to me when I ran across Teddy Roosevelt's "The Man in the Arena" speech:

> "It is not the critic who counts…The credit belongs to the man who is actually in the arena; whose face is marred by dust and sweat and blood; who, at the best, knows in the end the triumph of high achievement; and who, at worst, if he fails, at least fails while daring greatly; so that his place shall never be with those cold and timid souls who know neither victory or defeat."

My participation in the wrestling arena prepared me well for the business world and other aspects of life. Wrestling taught me the importance of developing strategies for dealing with problems and situations. Strategy is planning, preparing to win. The first component was to be prepared for any eventuality. The second was to get in great shape so as to never run out of gas, be tired at the end of a match, like I was in the first Muskingum match. A good example of my use of strategy was in the second Dickinson College match in my senior year. In the previous year, I hadn't used my legs in my match at Dickinson. In the match the following year, I decided to use my legs and tied the Dickinson Wrestler up in a figure four leg ride that he couldn't break and I handily won the match. After the match, one of the Dickinson wrestlers told me I had surprised them with my leg ride. My strategy had worked. The comment from the Dickinson wrestler made my day!

I didn't join a fraternity at W&J and didn't have much of a social life during college. My social life grew throughout the years and became somewhat respectable in my senior year. Work, going to school and wrestling kept me occupied. The jock fraternities—Phi Kappa Psi and Alpha Tau Omega—invited me to their parties. I was well-known on campus because of wrestling.

I became a member of the Letterman's Club in my sophomore year, having lettered in wrestling as a freshman. In my junior and senior years, I ran the concession stand at the football games for the Letterman's Club. This responsibility included selling advertising for the game program, selling the programs at the game and selling flowers at homecoming. I earned a lot of money for the Letterman's Club in the process. At one homecoming game, I took in more money for the Letterman's Club than the college did from ticket sales. This was a good experience for me. I got to help the club and do my duty as a member. I had never led such an effort that included a team of other lettermen, let alone planned and organized everything.

The concession stand sold soft drinks, candy bars, coffee, potato chips, etc. The first cold day presented a memorable event, an illustration that necessity is the mother of invention. In this case, it was innovation. The first cold game day was in November. We had a few games under our concession stand belt. All the previous game days had been warm, and we sold lots of soft drinks. On this cold day, hot coffee became the best seller. The coffee urn we had only made thirty cups. I quickly realized that we needed more coffee, and the coffee urn wasn't going to get the job dome.

The solution was to make instant coffee. I set one person to work boiling water in large pots. I was familiar with the area, so I sent another person down the street to the local grocery store to buy a case—maybe two cases—of instant coffee. We mixed instant coffee with the hot, sometimes boiling water. Not being a coffee drinker and never having made coffee before, I had no idea what it was supposed to taste like. We got some complaints, but the coffee was hot, and it was the only game in town. Talk about a monopoly; we sold a lot of coffee that day. I was better prepared for the next game. A bullet was successfully dodged.

In hindsight, I was very fortunate that Dave Scarborough, the Lettermen's Club faculty advisor and basketball coach, had faith in me to run the concession stand and manage other activities related to the football games. I had no experience for the job. But he convinced me I could do the job. I was very pleased with how I rose to the occasion.

I experienced some disappointments at W&J. I was bounced out of the engineering program. I thought I should have been named outstanding freshman wrestler but wasn't. I didn't get to go to the 4-I wrestling tournament that in previous years, conference champions had attended. My brothers weren't given financial aid by W&J and went elsewhere. There were other disappointments, but I learned something from each and look back fondly on my time there. It builds character, they say.

I still have a deep fondness and respect for the school and what it did for me. As I was about to leave for Rutgers graduate school, I ran into John Frazier at the Anchor Club on Route 40. He was in medical school and two years older than me. His dad and my dad had shot trap together. When he

Me receiving my W&J diploma from W&J President
Boyd C. Patterson

learned, I was going to go to Rutgers, he told me not to worry, that I was well prepared and could hold my own with the Ivy League and other big name schools. I soon found that John's forecast was right and still is today.

One evening during my junior year, I was a little depressed and my dad asked me what the problem was. I saw my chance to get some sympathy and poured my heart out about how tough it was to go to school, work twenty hours a week, wrestle and keep my grades up. My dad's response was, "You know, Ron, good things don't come easy." End of discussion. Not a lot of sympathy. Dad was a man of few words!

CHAPTER 18

MY EARLY YEARS OF EMPLOYMENT

At an early age, I began working in our ice cream business, mostly helping in the plant. When I got my driver's license around March of 1958, I began to do deliveries. My mother was in charge and supervised everything. Ice cream making is fairly simple. First, the ice cream mix was put in the machine. Then it was frozen like frozen custard, put in a carton and weighed. The cartons went in cases and were moved to the hardening room. It was my job and that of others to bring in the mix, the raw materials, weigh the cartons and take the cases to the freezer.

We were very proud of our product and competed on service—home delivery—and quality. It was difficult competing with big companies like Borden's, but we held our own. Our quality and delivery were tough to beat.

I also drove the truck and had an ice cream route delivering door to door on Saturdays during my W&J freshman year. I hated it. I was shy and didn't like asking people to buy my product. Selling doesn't come naturally to an introverted person. My brother Duane often went with me to help. Our standard line for new customers was, "Hi, I'm with Snee Ice Cream Company. We're building a delivery route through here. Do you folks eat ice cream?"

We also had some stores that bought ice cream wholesale. This often required my brothers and me delivering a 4-, 6-, 8- or 12-hole compartment ice cream freezer, which could be quite heavy, weighing as much as a soft drink machine. Coincidentally, every time we would deliver a freezer, we would run into someone with a bad back that couldn't help. We would have to unload and install the freezer by ourselves. Fortunately, we were strong, knew what we were doing and were up to the task. Dad taught us well.

In the second semester of my freshman year at W&J, I got a job as a room clerk at Washington Motel, which was just down the street from our dairy. I didn't like driving the ice cream truck and Dad wasn't driving me to school anymore. I decided to get a job and earn my own money.

The job paid a dollar an hour plus tips, which we were not supposed to accept but did. Dad let me drive the pickup truck to work and school if I paid for the gas. I worked twenty hours a week during school and forty hours a week during the summer. I saved my money and paid for all my tuition and books, with enough left over for spending on whatever I wanted. This job lasted from roughly April of my freshman year to December of my junior year, when I was fired for lack of work even though I had seniority over the two other guys who weren't laid off. I never understood the logic in that decision. I had reduced my schedule to one day a week to accommodate wrestling practice and the boss apparently didn't like it. He told one of my colleagues to tell me not to come in anymore. He didn't have the guts to tell me himself.

The next few months were lean. In April of my junior year, I got a job at the Coca-Cola plant at a $1.25 per hour, a twenty-five percent raise! I held that job until I left for graduate school at Rutgers University in New Brunswick, New Jersey. I sorted bottles, packed pallets off the production line and cleaned the men's and women's restrooms, etc. As they grew confident in my work, I was given the responsibility of delivering in a pickup truck. On occasion, I drove one of the large, empty trucks to the plant.

The plant was run by the Cameron Brothers: Pete, Dick and Donnie, the third generation of their family to own and operate the company. Pete and I became particularly fond of each other and kept in touch over the years. He was a tough taskmaster but very fair. He had played middle guard on Woody Hays' football team at Denison while in college. Woody Hays went on to be a very successful coach at Ohio State University.

Pete had also studied regression analysis in college and had an idea what statistics was about. One day while stacking pallets of sugar some forty feet high, he criticized my stacking speed, saying, "Come on, Snee! My grandmother could stack pallets faster than that." My slow speed was due to my vision of a forty-foot stack of pallets of sugar falling over. This would NOT have been a pretty sight and Pete would have been very angry, to say the least.

Pete's daughter Gwen went to the University of Delaware to study business. She subsequently went to work for DuPont in finance for a few years prior to returning to the family business. Pete wrote me a letter and told me about Gwen working at DuPont. I contacted her to touch base. We had a nice chat, agreeing that both of us would go out of our way to buy a Coke rather than settle for the other brand.

I subsequently visited Pete to say hello. He took me down to the stable to see his prize trotter that had recently won a big race. Pete told me he'd been offered a hundred thousand dollars for the horse after winning the big race. He said, "There were two fools present that day: the one that made the offer and the one that turned it down." I like this story and tell it often.

I had the good fortune to be at the celebration when the Cameron family was awarded the 1993 W&J Entrepreneur of the Year Award. I was proud of the Cameron family and honored to be invited. I was pleased to later receive the 2020 W&J Entrepreneur of Year Award. In later years, two of my brother Tom's boys, Ryan and Jeff, worked at the Coke plant. On more than one occasion over the years, Pete delighted in telling Tom, much to his displeasure, that there was only one good Snee: Ron! On a Thursday in September, I quit my job at the Coke plant and drove the next day to New Brunswick, New Jersey, to start the next phase of my life: graduate work in statistics.

CHAPTER 19

OUR VEHICLES

The first car I recall Mom and Dad owning was a '50 Ford. This was followed by a red and black '53 Mercury, a white '58 Mercury, a '60 Nash Rambler and a '63 Ford Fairlane. There was also a series of pickup trucks, both Fords and Chevys. The Chevys were often purchased from Tom Mankey, who ran a garage in Amity and sold Chevrolets. Dad liked to support local businesses when he could. Mom drove the family car and Dad drove the pickup truck. He liked it that way. When it snowed, Dad liked to load the truck bed with snow. The added weight enabled him to drive almost anywhere. Mom always took care of maintenance, including getting the cars and trucks greased and the oil changed.

The '53 Mercury was a good, sharp car and when it was time, they decided to get another Mercury, a 1958 model. One day when Mom and Dad were coming home, the '58 Mercury caught fire. The car was in the garage for almost a month. It never ran right again, and Dad traded it for a '60 Nash Rambler that was a tin can on wheels, a big mistake. That car was replaced with a white '63 Ford Fairlane. Dad was a big fan of Ford. GM was too big as far as he was concerned. I was also loyal to Ford and only abandoned them in 1980 when their quality decreased. I have yet to buy another Ford!

I've seen a lot of changes in automobiles over the years. Tire mileage was one of them and was a huge improvement. In the fifties and sixties, tires lasted less than 25,000 miles. Mom frequently purchased recapped tires for about seven dollars each. By 1999, we routinely got 50,000 miles from tires. Flat tires were also frequent. By 1999, flats were rare. Gas had increased from $.26 cents per gallon to $1.20-$1.40 per gallon. Self-service gas stations, popular in 1999, were unheard of in the fifties. The 1973 oil crisis changed all of that. Today, the roads are much better, cars are built better and we can drive a lot faster: 70 mph in 1999 versus 50 mph back then.

When I graduated from W&J, I had the money and decided it was time to buy a car. With no help or guidance from my parents, I bought a used '56 Ford for five hundred dollars from a used car dealer in Canonsburg. I paid the asking price, as I didn't know how to negotiate. I always wanted a '56 Ford and now I had one. Two tries blew out on a double date with Jimmy Pareso. Fortunately, we were in Washington after being in Pittsburgh, and Jimmy's dad came to pick us up.

I drove that car to Rutgers and back home several times. I had riders to and from New Jersey to help with the expenses. I think the going rate was ten to fifteen dollars per person. I usually took two or three riders. I never made any money from the riders, though, due to repairs that tended to eat up the money. I remember replacing a starter, a battery, a distributor cap, headlights, an oil cap and other things. None of my friends and family liked my car and repeatedly told me it was too old to make the trip back and forth from New Brunswick to Amity.

In May of 1965, I gave in to the pressure and bought a 1965 Ford Falcon that I drove for seventeen years! Characteristically, I traded in my beloved '56 Ford and took what they gave me. I still didn't know how to negotiate and there was no one to help me. The Falcon cost me about two thousand dollars after the trade-in. I had two thousand dollars in the bank but decided to borrow about two hundred dollars from Mom so I wouldn't empty my bank account completely. I paid her back in a few months. I never purchased a used car again. I also never traded cars again. I subsequently sold my old cars privately.

I was naïve in those days. I lost my license plate for the '56 Ford during one of my trips to New Jersey. On the advice of my mother, I ordered another plate from Harrisburg and carried a notarized affidavit stating that I had lost the plate and another was forthcoming. Well, the plate didn't come, and I continued to drive the car. One night I was stopped by a township policeman who, after listening to my story, impounded my car, drove me to the edge of New Brunswick and left me to walk the rest of the way. It was a short distance, but he didn't know that. He wasn't going to give me any ride at all except I had no one to pick me up. It cost me fifty dollars for towing and more for a set of New Jersey license plates and driver's license.

On another occasion, I had a small fender bender on ice and the insurance company wanted to cancel my insurance. Manny Morris, our insurance agent and lifelong family friend, wrote Kemper Insurance, telling them how great I was and how they should hire me rather than cancel my insurance. When I got married in 1967, Manny sent me a letter telling me it was now time to get my insurance in New Jersey, which I did.

CHAPTER 20

LESSONS LEARNED

Mom always taught us to save at every opportunity. She was raised during the depression, and it left an impression on her. She passed that impression on to her boys. We saved money from sheep sales, birthday and Christmas gifts, garden vegetable and walnut sales, money from odd jobs and regular jobs, etc.

As noted previously, I had two thousand dollars in the bank when I bought my 1965 Ford Falcon. This was after buying my '56 Ford and paying for my last three years of college. I had no debts and was very proud of it. I continued to be a saver throughout my life. The only debt I've had was a house mortgage and an occasional car loan.

I followed Mom's philosophy of saving and not going into debt, perhaps to a fault. I was awarded a half-tuition scholarship by W&J, and a loan to cover the other half of the tuition. I was taught not to borrow money unless I had to, so I worked and saved my money and never accepted the loan even though it didn't have to be repaid until after graduation. In hindsight, which is always 20-20, I should have taken the loan, saved my money and paid off the loan when I had to start paying interest. At least I had the peace of mind of not being in debt, a very old-fashioned philosophy today.

I also add here my first-grade teacher, Mrs Elliott's admonishment: "don't waste time. Wasted time is lost and gone forever. I keep this in mind every day to make the best use of the time I have on God's green earth.

CHAPTER 21

LEAVING THE FARM

I worked up to the last minute at Coca-Cola to earn as much money as possible. I had never lived on my own. I had no idea how much it would cost. Could I live in high-cost New Jersey on a teaching assistantship paying twenty-two hundred dollars for nine months? I was going to an area I had never been, a highly urbanized area, probably without a farm in sight. Or so I thought. While I didn't think about it at the time, I was leaving all I had known and loved up to that point in my life: the Coke plant, Washington, Amity, and all of western Pennsylvania. Most significant of all, I was leaving my family, friends, and our farm.

I left at about 8:00 a.m. on a Friday morning in early September 1963. Everything I owned was in my car: my clothes hung on a pole across the back seat and books, etc. in the trunk. I had no place to stay when I got to Rutgers. Mom told me to stay at the YMCA until I found a place. I arrived at the Rutgers Statistics Center around 2:00 p.m. There I met Miss Vicky Tally, secretary to the department head, Dr. Ellis Ott. She asked if I had a place to stay. When I told her I didn't, she said she knew just the place: a third-floor walkup apartment on George Street, two doors from where she lived, a couple of blocks from the Rutgers Douglas College campus. So, by 5:00 p.m. on Friday, I had a place to live and continued to live there for the next four years. Someone was surely looking after me.

The next weekend, I attended the Rutgers Quality Conference at the insistence of Dr. Ott. I had no idea what they were talking about at the conference. Little did I know that in a year or so, it would be my life's work. A few weeks after that, I began graduate school classes and teaching math in the Rutgers night school. I was the youngest one in the class. My new life was underway. But that's another story for another time.

EPILOGUE

So, you ask, whatever happened to this guy who grew up on a farm in western Pennsylvania?

I kept learning, growing, and developing. I followed my interest in mathematics and went on to graduate school at Rutgers University. There, I earned MS and PhD degrees in Applied and Mathematical Statistics. I was also a teaching assistant in the Statistics Center, research assistant, and assistant professor at the Rutgers University College of Agriculture and Environmental Science. This assignment took me back to my roots in agriculture.

At this point in my career, I decided to get some industrial experience. I accepted an assignment in the DuPont's Applied Statistics Group in Newark, Delaware, and moved through several roles including manager. One major assignment was at Haskell Laboratory for Toxicology and Industrial Medicine, where I worked on studies of rats, mice, guinea pigs, dogs, and humans. Much of what I learned on the farm directly applied to the studies.

At DuPont, after managing part of the Applied Statistics Group, I moved on to manage a group on engineers and geologists in the Engineering Services Division at the Beaumont, Texas, plant. I concluded my DuPont career as quality manager in DuPont's Project Engineering Division and leader of the DuPont Corporate Improvement Curriculum. My DuPont work was recognized by five DuPont performance excellence awards.

I took early retirement from DuPont to pursue a management consulting career. I served as management consultant and vice president at Joiner Associates, a Deming Based Business Improvement Consulting Company. This was followed by a two-year stint as vice president, process assurance, at Bell Atlantic, which is now Verizon. I then entered the Lean Six Sigma consulting business, working with Sigma Breakthrough Technologies, Inc. (process improvement leader, 1998-2001) and Tunnell Consulting, Inc. (principal, 2001-2008). I retired from Tunnell Consulting and reenergized Snee Associates, LLC, which was founded in 1998.

The focus of my consulting work since 1998 has been process and organizational improvement for the pharmaceutical and biotechnology industries. As of 2022, I have helped thirty-two organizations make major improvements in their performance. In addition to my consulting work, I have maintained an active research program and speaking career that has resulted in coauthoring eight books and more than three hundred thirty published articles. I have received numerous awards, including Elected American Society for Quality Honorary Member, American Statistical Association Deming Lectureship, and the Washington and Jefferson College 2020 Entrepreneur of Year Award, as well as more than thirty other professional awards. Along the way, my work has had a combined focus on statistics, improvement, leadership, and management. Sports, particularly wrestling, agriculture, education, improvement, and statistical thinking, have remained lifelong interests.

They say it takes a village to raise a child. That has certainly been the case in my experience. I'm honored to acknowledge the many persons in the villages I've had the opportunity of being a member. My deep thanks to all who have helped me along the way. And last but not least, I acknowledge the benefits of growing up on the farm: hard work, how to work, focus, loyalty and discipline, all contribute to a successful life.

ACKNOWLEDGEMENTS

Many persons contributed to stories contained in this book. It is a pleasure to acknowledge their contributions. Some persons deserve special acknowledgement. It all began with my parents, Rolland Davis and Helene Weber Snee. They provided leadership, guidance and support for the many educational, farm and business experiences I describe.

My brothers Tom and Duane who were coconspirators in the many ventures and adventures I talk about. Our times together, the good, the bad and the ugly will fondly be remembered.

My teachers at Amity Elementary School, Trinity High School and Washington and Jefferson College got me started on my learning process which continues today. Learning and the associated new experiences continue to be one of the major sources of my joy in life.

Edith Wright Crouse, Karen Kreps DelGrosso, Donald Dunbar, and Lynne Hare commented on earlier versions of this book that provided insights and clarity which greatly improved the presentation of my story.

The help and guidance of Publisher. Lois Hoffman, the founder of the Happy Self-Publisher, and Editor Susan Sutphin greatly contributed to improving the exposition in this book and making it a reality.

The photo on the back cover of this book is of the Snee Beef Cattle Farm located south of Amity, PA. The Snee Farm, owned and operated by Duane and Valerie Snee, breeds some of the most highly prized Simmental beef cattle in the industry. The photo was provided by Duane C. Snee

ABOUT THE AUTHOR

Ron Snee is a management consultant, researcher, speaker, and teacher. He grew up on a farm in southwestern Pennsylvania and began his formal education in a one-room school: one teacher, fifty students in four grades, with a pot belly stove for heat, water pump out front for drinking water and outhouses in the rear. He started his career working at The DuPont company in a variety of positions prior to launching his consulting career. He has also served on the faculties of Rutgers, Temple and Delaware universities.

Ron has written several books and articles focusing on organizational and quality improvement, management, leadership, statistical thinking and college wrestling. His work has received global acclaim and been recognized with numerous awards and honors. With a focus on learning, he continues to practice his craft using the principles and values he learned on the farm and throughout his career. He resides with his wife Marjorie in Newark, Delaware. His daughters Jennifer and Victoria and Granddaughter Mary live in the Dallas, Texas area.

Made in the USA
Middletown, DE
09 July 2023

34503325R00076